Travel Allenways *Always*

A Pictorial History Of Allenways Coaches

Travel
Allenways
Always

A Pictorial History Of Allenways Coaches

Andrew Roberts

BREWIN BOOKS

Published by Brewin Books Ltd
Studley, Warwickshire B80 7LG
in 2006

www.brewinbooks.com

ISBN 1 85858 277 6

British Library Cataloguing in Publication Data
A Catalogue record for this book is available from the British Library.

Typeset in Times
Printed in Great Britain by
Alden Press Limited.

Contents

*"Travel by Motor Coach for health's sake" -
an early handbill advertising the service to
Weston-super-Mare.*

*An early leaflet for the service to Skegness
- the service to this resort was started in the late
1930's to coincide with the opening of Butlin's
first holiday camp.*

An example of the company letterhead in use in the late 1940's and 1950's.

Allenways Coaches 1928 - 1992

"Travel Allenways - Always" was the slogan used by one of Birmingham's pioneer coach operators.

George Edward Allen started Allenways in the late 1920's and, over the next 64 years, the company would become one of the largest coach operators in the City of Birmingham.

Mr Allen's first coach was a Leyland Lioness with 26-seat Buckingham body bought new in March 1928. The following year, four more new coaches were purchased; again all 26-seat Buckingham bodied Leyland Lionesses. The livery of these vehicles was cream and green and all five saw about twenty years service with Allenways. Mr Allen was particularly proud of the 1928 vehicle, which, by 1935 had covered around 230,000 miles, and the engine still had the original pistons and had not been re-bored. The 1929 vehicles all received new bodies in 1938 by Holbrook.

The company originally operated from 162 Darwin Street in Balsall Heath but in 1936 moved to 88 Tindal Street also in Balsall Heath. Around this time a limited company "Allenways Limited" was formed and a holiday coach service to the recently opened Butlins holiday camp at Skegness was started. This would be the start of a long association with Butlins, as over the years Allenways established a series of summer services serving many of that companies holiday centres.

After the Second World War, the company moved again to 580 Moseley Road. These premises were located next to the Corporation tram depot and included a booking office and maintenance garage. A large plot of land, on the opposite side of the road, was also owned and was used for parking the fleet of coaches.

Mr Allen sold the business in 1948 to the Weatherhogg family. The new managing director was Mr Tom Weatherhogg and his son Tom Weatherhogg junior was also a director. A Mr A B Davidson was also a Director and Traffic Manager but by 1953 this role had been taken by Mr AT Perkins - known as "Major Perkins".

Pictures of Allenways premises have been hard to find, but the Moseley Road garage and booking office can just be seen in the background of this photograph of trainee mechanic Gordon Harborne who is polishing his first car, a 1934 Austin 16. G Harborne collection

This picture shows several coaches in the open parking area opposite the garage - on the corner of Moseley Road and Cromer Road. Roy Marshall collection

The Weatherhogg family were no strangers to transport, having operated a haulage business until nationalisation; the origins of which went back to the 1920s when a milk round was started using a horse and cart. In addition to Allenways, the family also owned a company called Storage and Haulage Limited that was based on Amington Road in Yardley. The main part of this business involved the storage of Austin cars in CKD kit form. Most of the cars produced by Austin for export in this manner were handled and space was leased at Warehouses at various sites including Elmdon Airport, The British Industries Fair at Castle Bromwich and at a former air base at Honeybourne. The kits were stacked in boxes 5 or 6 high and then transported to various ports for exportation. Other lorries were also operated on contract to Kellogg's and the Castrol Oil Company. At some time, the family also owned Ashfield Motors in Moseley - a Vauxhall car dealership.

Apart from the Leylands acquired new in 1928 and 1929, most other coach fleet additions of the 1930's and early 1940's were second-hand, although a Leyland TS6 was bought new in 1934 and a Mulliner bodied Bedford OWB in 1943. The Weatherhogg family however quickly replaced most of the coaches, with nine new vehicles purchased during 1948 and 1949. Most had Guy chassis but there were also some Leylands and a Commer Commando. Fleet numbers were applied to all vehicles until the early 1950's and many of the coaches purchased new in 1949 and the early 1950's also received names.

As an experiment, two extremely unusual coaches were added to the fleet in 1950; both had a Foden PVFE6 chassis with two-stroke engine and bodywork built by the Lincolnshire Trailer Company. At the time, the highest capacity single-deck coach available seated around 33 passengers. The Fodens were designed to carry 43 passengers to a patented design by George Crelin. The seats were arranged face-to-face - similar to a railway carriage on two levels but served by just one gangway. This apparently caused some problems with the traffic commissioners who could not decide whether these vehicles should comply with single or double deck regulations. Eventually they were licensed as "half-deckers" - although it is not sure which set of regulations they had to comply with! Marketed as "Pullman" coaches, they created a great deal of press attention and a ceremony was held on June 9th to officially name them "City of Birmingham" and "City of Lincoln". This took place at the Chateau Impney

Hotel in Droitwich and as well as being reported by local and trade press, Pathe News filmed the event. Although revolutionary in design and concept they proved to be unsuccessful in operation - mainly because passengers did not like sitting facing each other, or with their backs to the front of the coach. Both had left the fleet by 1958, one was damaged in an accident and ended its days, after being re-built by Allenways, as a Kellogg's Corn Flake delivery lorry.

More conventional coaches were chosen for all future purchases with three Burlingham Seagull bodied vehicles acquired in 1951, two on Leyland Royal Tiger chassis and the other on AEC Regal IV. The Commer Avenger chassis was also favoured with many Plaxton bodied examples being purchased throughout the 1950's. The livery at this time was changed to grey and green.

During the mid 1950's a licence was granted to operate from Birmingham's Elmdon Airport to anywhere in England or Wales. This was obtained in response to a request from Airlines operating from the Airport for Allenways to provide passenger transfers in the event of diverted flights owing to bad weather. This arrangement continued for many years and at times as many as 50 coach loads of passengers could be transferred in any one-day.

Also in the 1950's a yard was acquired at 7 - 9 Park Street. Located opposite the Bull Ring in the city centre this was to become known as "The Bull Ring Coach Station". A haulage company called Gupwells had previously used these premises, and Allenways had a three-bay maintenance garage built on the site. An office building was also erected using an ex-council prefab which is believed to have cost £120.00 and was constructed by Allenways staff using a rope and coach to pull the framework in place.

Besides operating coaches from Park Street, the garage also carried out car repairs and was one of the first in Birmingham to be appointed as an M.O.T. testing station. A car hire service was also operated as well as a driving school called West End School of Motoring, which used a fleet of Morris 1000 saloons. One disadvantage of the city centre location was that on occasions, cattle from the nearby Bull Ring market escaped and strayed down Park Street into Allenways yard!

Throughout the 1950's and 1960's, in addition to private hire and summer holiday

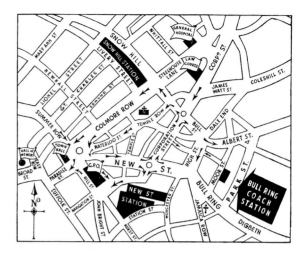

This map, showing the location of the "Bull Ring Coach Station" was printed in the company's brochures.

services, excursions formed a major part of the company's activities. Day, half-day and evening trips were popular and Allenways also served many race meetings around the country. All coaches departed from Allenways own departure stand on Station Street and passengers would be transferred to there from other pick-up points in the city. The company owned two taxis - an Armstrong Siddeley and an Austin 18, These were painted in the same colours as the coach fleet and were used to transfer passengers to the coach departure point. Bookings were accepted at a network of agents, which interestingly included several located in resorts served by the company's summer express services thus enabling residents of those resorts to travel to the Midlands.

Inclusive holidays were offered but not on a great scale, many were based around the express services with local excursions being provided by resort based operators. The 1952 brochure featured such "Pleasure Planned Holidays" to Weston and North Devon operated in conjunction with Wems Luxury Coaches of Weston-Super-Mare. The same brochure also featured continental holidays operated by Imperial Motorways (Birmingham) Limited, who were in fact based in Bromsgrove. A 16-day "Grand European" tour, including Bavaria, The Tyrol, Dolomites and Switzerland cost £48.00. Another interesting service advertised was a weekly service from Allenways Bull Ring Coach Station to Paris for £10.00 return, this too was operated by Imperial Motorways.

The first continental journey was operated in 1960 to Rome. Allenways driver, Gordon Harborne, is pictured with the tour guide and Sealandair Coaches' driver Alan. The coach was 4462 VP, a Ford Thames 570E with Duple Yeoman body new that year. G Harborne collection

Allenways first journey abroad was made in 1960, when one of their coaches travelled with another from the Sealandair of West Bromwich fleet to Rome. The tour was undertaken on behalf of Longmeadow Girls School in Birmingham and would herald the start of many future International journeys for the company, most noteworthy of which would be a regular tour to the Soviet Union. The first departure of this 2,500 mile tour was made in 1963 with a 41-seat Duple Trooper bodied Ford Thames 570E. Throughout the 1970's and 1980's regular Continental tours were also operated for a company called Schools Travel Service. This involved Allenways vehicles collecting passengers from all parts of the country as well as transporting other groups who were visiting the U.K.

Contract work also provided valuable and regular work for the fleet, and licences were held to transport workers to the BSA factory at Redditch, G.E.C. at Witton and Reynolds Tubes. Another contract involved three or four coaches each day from Birmingham and the Tamworth

area to and from Hams Hall Power Station near Coleshill. Some vehicles were utilised during the day, in between works contracts, for school transport. When Alfred Bird relocated its factory in Deritend to Banbury, Allenways transported workers there and back each day. This contracted lasted for about two years. Weekend journeys were also undertaken on behalf of the Armed Forces to transport personnel to Catterick camp.

The coach fleet received five new Duple Yeoman bodied Ford Thames in 1960. These vehicles introduced a new livery described as "Alpine Mauve and Mushroom". Further Duple bodied Ford Thames coaches were purchased during the following three years as well as four Bedford VALs - one with Duple body and three with Plaxton bodies. The "Alpine Mauve" was applied in a darker shade from 1963 and some red was also added to the livery.

A separate contract fleet was established in the early 1960's that comprised entirely of used vehicles - some of which were transferred from the main Allenways fleet. These vehicles were operated as "non-psv" and worked on contract to British Railways to transport maintenance workers. This arrangement ended in 1971.

The company made a move into the travel business in 1964 when a travel office was set-up in association with Butlins at the newly opened Bull Ring shopping centre. This joint venture dealt with Butlin's reservations and Allenways Coach bookings. Allenways held licences for services to Skegness, Pwllheli and later Minehead all of which served the Butlins holiday centres at those resorts. Other routes included Weston, Great Yarmouth and Lowestoft and a North Wales service covered Rhyl, Llandudno and Colwyn Bay. Most routes were licensed from Birmingham pick-up points but some were also available from Wolverhampton. The Skegness service was the most popular route and pick-up points in Birmingham, Lichfield, Tamworth, Wolverhampton, Bilston, West Bromwich and Ashby-de-la-Zouch were authorised. In the heyday years of coach travel, Allenways were one of the major providers of summer coastal services and demand was such that many coaches, in addition to the company's own, were hired from operators across the Midlands each weekend. The Travel office was later developed to become a full travel agency and in the early 1980's was re-located to one of the retail units below the multi-storey car park - opposite St.Martins Church.

In 1965 a joint venture was started with the Ryland Vehicle Group whereby Allenways provided tankers and drivers for fuel deliveries. A separate company "Hire Services (Birmingham) Limited" was set-up for this enterprise. The busiest time for this business was during the winter months, this coincided with the quieter time for the coach operation and, after training some coach drivers were employed to drive tankers until the start of the new coaching season. This operation was very successful and by 1970 over 50 vehicles were being supplied, its success however began to effect the Allenways' coaching operations and the Weatherhogg family decided to relinquish their interest in the business. Allenways did however continue to operate a small fleet of their own tankers mainly involved with the delivery of heating oil.

The Ford R-series chassis with Plaxton bodywork became the choice for all vehicle purchases from 1968 until 1982. Most were bought new and were built to Allenways specification which included a "Telma" magnetic retarder, automatic chassis lubrication and extra capacity fuel tanks (70 gallons) - necessary for the long continental journeys operated. The Plaxton bodywork featured a power operated entrance door, public address system, radio cassette and illuminated side name panels. Full capacity luggage lockers were also incorporated and later bodies also had curtains, tinted windows and "Bristol" type front name domes.

In 1970 Paul Weatherhogg, son of Tom Weatherhogg junior, became Managing Director - he was assisted in the running of the company by General Manager Ray Taylor and Fleet Maintenance Manager, Lenn Nunn - both of whom gave long service to the company.

1973 saw considerable expansion when the business of Superb Coaches (Birmingham) Limited was acquired. CF Cantello, who started trading in 1956 as Radley Motors, previously owned this business. Mr Cantello acquired Superb Coaches in 1964 and in 1969 also acquired Mason's Coachways of Darlaston, which was re-named Mason's - Superb. The Birmingham based Superb Coaches and Darlaston Mason-Superb continued to be run separate from the Allenways fleet until 1975. Further details of Radley Motors and Superb Coaches can be found on page 74.

An A.B.T.A. travel agency was added to the Allenways business portfolio in 1974 when Simmonds Travel Agency on Church Road in Yardley was acquired. The name was changed to Allenways Travel and, in 1981, the business moved to a new shop on Church Road in the centre of the Yew Tree shopping area.

By 1975, with the acquisition of Superb Coaches and its associated fleets, the number of coaches operated had grown to over 40 vehicles. At this time the only working director of the business was Paul Weatherhogg who considered that the company had expanded too large for just one person to look after properly. The business was re-organised to comprise three subsidiary companies - Allenways Coaches Ltd, Allenways Travel Ltd and Allenways Vehicle Hire Ltd. The Mason's of Darlaston licenses and premises were sold to Fred Winkle (Pathfinder Tours) of Willenhall who still trades today as "Pathfinder-Masons". The Allenways coach fleet moved to the former Superb Coaches depot at 10 Fortnum

Close in Tile Cross. The remaining Superb Coaches fleet was amalgamated with Allenways but most of the acquired vehicles were sold at the end of 1975.

Day excursions had formed a major part of the Allenways business in the early years but by 1975 this part of the companies activities only accounted for about 15% of the total operations. The restricted pick-up points on the licences became difficult to serve economically, so this part of the business was sold to Everton's Coaches of Droitwich who had also recently acquired the excursion licences of Andy's Coaches of Birmingham.

During 1976 negotiations were started to sell the company to West Midlands Passenger Transport. This was as a result of the P.T.E.'s private hire department's desire to establish a coaching fleet. The proposed sale was however blocked by the Passenger Transport Authority and the Weatherhogg family continued to run Allenways.

In 1977 the depot at 7 - 9 Park Street was sold to Wallace Arnold who, at the time, had a dedicated West Midlands British Tour programme. Park Street was used as their Midlands headquarters and Birmingham departure point. Initially no coaches were based in Birmingham with vehicles just parked there overnight - between tour departures. This however changed in 1980 when Wallace Arnold became involved with the British Coachways consortium - the post de-regulation challenge to National Express. Up to four coaches were operated out of Birmingham on a daily service to and from London. Other destinations available included Glasgow, Manchester, Swansea and Bristol. These were served by other British Coachways members' vehicles that called at Park Street en-route, including Parks of Hamilton, Grey Green, Shearings, Morris Brothers of Swansea and Warner's of Tewkesbury. During their occupation of the premises, Wallace Arnold rented out space to the car hire company Avis who took over the site when W.A. abandoned its Midlands operations in 1981. Allenways continued to use Park Street as a departure point for their summer Express Services, and the Wallace Arnold booking office was appointed as a booking agent.

In 1978, an experimental service was started, when a stage carriage licence was granted to the

company to operate between Birmingham and East Midlands Airport. The licence was restricted to pre-booked passengers and was marketed through Allenways own travel shops and other travel agents. The service was scheduled around holiday flights operated by Horizon, Thomson and Intasun Holidays and boarding points were available in Birmingham, Erdington, Sutton Coldfield, Lichfield, Tamworth, Measham and Ashby-de-la-Zouch. Return departures were linked to particular holiday flights so that in the event of a delay the coach waited for the arrival of the flight.

Allenways had purchased their first Ford based coaches in 1961 and during the following years more than 50 of the type were acquired, from the Thames Trader 570E and 676E through to the "R" series of the 1960's, 70's and 80's - the last of the make were two R1114s purchased in 1982. Although they had received excellent service from these vehicles, the increased amount of long-distance continental work led to a change to Volvo. The first arrived new in late 1981 and was followed by a nearly new example in 1982. Two Jonckheere bodied B10Ms, purchased in 1984, were however the last new coaches acquired by the company under the ownership of the Weatherhogg family.

In 1986 the family, shareholders and directors took the decision to cease operating coaches. The company, and the Fortnum Close depot was sold to David Watkiss who operated Claribel Coaches - no vehicles were involved as these were disposed of separately. Claribel moved their fleet to Fortnum Close and ran Allenways as a separate business but on a smaller scale than its previous owners. Two Duple 425 coaches were acquired new, one in 1987 and the other in 1989, in a silver and red livery with Allenways fleet name. Although other vehicles were licensed to Allenways, they were in Claribel livery or just plain white. The Allenways travel agency at Yardley was sold to James Travel, and Wellvale Travel acquired the City centre shop.

The Watkiss family closed the Allenways part of their business in 1992 thus ending 64 years of Birmingham' coaching history. The family today continues to operate their fleet of modern Claribel buses on stage carriage routes in Birmingham, as well as around four Bova Futuras under the Birmingham International Coaches name.

1929 - VP 9142, Leyland Lioness chassis with handsome 26-seat Buckingham body. Four identical coaches were acquired new in this year and were to operate in the Allenways fleet for many years. Note the full-length sunshine roof and the luggage storage area at the rear of the roof. The company was originally based in Darwin Street in Bordesley Green. G Harborne collection

All of the 1929 Leyland Lionesses were re-bodied in 1938 by Holbrook. VP 9143 is pictured shortly after completion and displays fleet number 3 - fleet numbers were used until the early 1950's. After its passenger carrying service, Allenways converted this vehicle into a breakdown tender.
Roy Marshall collection

An offside view of another Leyland Lioness - VP 9141. These vehicles remained in service with Allenways for around twenty years - Mr Allen apparently preferred the bonneted design to more modern "half-cab" coaches. RHG Simpson

1934 - AOF 191, Leyland TS6 chassis with elegant Burlingham 32-seat bodywork. Note the rear passenger entrance, curtains, and glazed cove panels - luxury travel 1930's style. This coach was re-bodied by Allenways in 1949. Roy Marshall collection

Another view of AOF 191 with passengers boarding a private hire journey - this picture is believed to be taken on the Moseley Road in Birmingham, opposite Allenways garage and booking office. Roy Marshall collection

1936 - BOX 499, Maudslay SF40 chassis with 32-seat Burlingham "Airflow" body. Although still a front engine design, the position of the front axle allowed the forward position of the passenger door. This combined with the streamline body created a very modern looking coach for the period. The coach served the Allenways fleet until 1954. A Roberts collection

1948 - JOH 155, Leyland TS2 chassis with 33-seat bodywork by NMU. This vehicle was acquired from Noakes of Pensnett with original registration TY 4495 and with a different body. Before entering service with Allenways in 1948, the chassis was re-bodied and the re-furbished coach was re-registered - as above. Roy Marshall collection

Leyland Lioness coach, VP 9143 was withdrawn from passenger carrying service in the late 1940's and was converted by Allenways into a breakdown tender. It served the company for many years in this guise before being replaced by a converted Fire Engine. In this view, the vehicle is seen at the Park Street depot - parked next to the garage building. PM Photography

EXPRESS SERVICES
1949

Service No. 1.

PWLLHELI. SATURDAYS ONLY.
Period of Operation:

OUTWARDS.   INWARDS.
April 16th to Sept. 24th, 1949.   April 23rd to October 1st, 1949.

Time and Fare Table.

		Return Fare
580, Moseley Road	7.45 a.m.	36/-
Smithfield Garage	8.00 a.m.	36/-
Don Everall's Garage, Wolverhampton	8.40 a.m.	33/3
Pwllheli	2.00 p.m.	

Pwllheli	3.00 p.m.
Don Everall's Garage, Wolverhampton	8.05 p.m.
Smithfield Garage	8.45 p.m.
580, Moseley Road	8.50 p.m.

Children over 4 years and under 14 years, half fare.

Service No. 2.

FILTON & WESTON-SUPER-MARE. SATURDAYS ONLY.
Period of Operation:

OUTWARDS.   INWARDS.
June 4th to Sept. 4th, 1949.   June 11th to Sept. 11th, 1949.

Time and Fare Table.

		Single	Period Return
Dale End Coach Station	9.00 a.m.		
Filton	12.45 p.m.	9/3	15/3
Weston-Super-Mare	1.45 p.m.	11/-	19/3

Weston-Super-Mare (Melrose Café)	3.30 p.m.
Filton	4.30 p.m.
Dale End Coach Station	8.20 p.m.

Children over 4 years and under 14 years, half fare.

Travel Allenways Always!

'Phone CALthorpe 3191   580, MOSELEY ROAD, BIRMINGHAM, 12

1949 leaflet for Express Coach services. Destinations included Pwllheli, Filton and Weston-super-Mare, Boston, Wainfleet and Skegness, Cambridge, Great Yarmouth and Lowestoft, Harwich and Dovercourt. All were operated on Saturday but a service to Great Yarmouth was also offered on Friday and a Sunday service to Skegness was available during peak holiday periods.

1949 - JOH 880, Guy Arab III chassis with 33-seat Barnard body - one of four purchased this year. This coach received fleet number 18 and was named "Warwick Castle" - a number of coaches were named in the late 1940's and early 1950's. Roy Marshall collection

1950 - KOC 662, one of the two unusual "half-deck" Foden - Pullman coaches to join the fleet in this year. Both were based on a Foden PVF6 chassis and seated 43 passengers within the Lincs Trailer body. This coach was named "City of Birmingham" and carried fleet number 23. Roy Marshall collection

A ceremony to name both of the Foden coaches was held at the Chateau Impney Hotel in Droitwich on June 9th 1950. The event was reported in local and trade press as well as being featured in "Pathe News". In this view guests and staff pose for the camera with both coaches. R Steele collection

Education Minister, Sir Edward Boyle, christens KOC 662 "City of Birmingham" with traditional champagne. The speedometer of these vehicles was unusually located in the centre of the large white steering wheel. R Steele collection

These three rare interior views of one of the Lines - Trailer "Pullman" Coaches provide an impression of the unusual layout of these vehicles. The seats on both levels were reached by one gangway. ITN Archive / stills

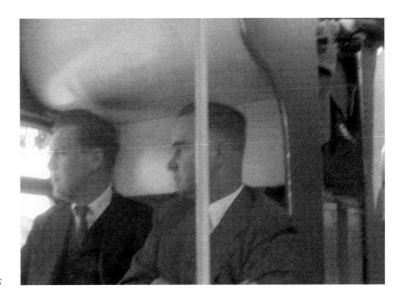

Passengers seated in the lower level seats sat beneath those on the upper level. ITN Archive / stills

The seats were arranged in sets of four - facing each other. Passengers apparently did not like this arrangement - not wishing to sit facing each other, or with their backs to the front of the coach. ITN Archive / stills

A nearside view of KOC 663 "City of Lincoln" - note the small door above the front wheel ahead of the main entrance. The destination blind reads, "Races" - Allenways operated many excursions to horse and dog race meetings. PM Photography

Another view of KOC 663. The body design was patented by Mr George Crelin and Lincs Trailer produced eleven similar bodies between 1949 and 1951 before they went out of business. Mann Egerton acquired the patent and built around nine more on various chassis. Allenways later converted KOC 663 into a van. Roy Marshall collection

1950 - KOC 665, Commer Avenger I chassis with 33-seat Plaxton body. The destinations painted on the window louvres read: England, Holland, Switzerland, Spain, Italy - the first continental journey by an Allenways coach was some 10 years later! Roy Marshall collection

Another view of KOC 665, pictured at Epsom. This coach received fleet number 26 and was named "Windsor Castle". It was one of the first Plaxton bodied coaches purchased. NA3T / ATPH

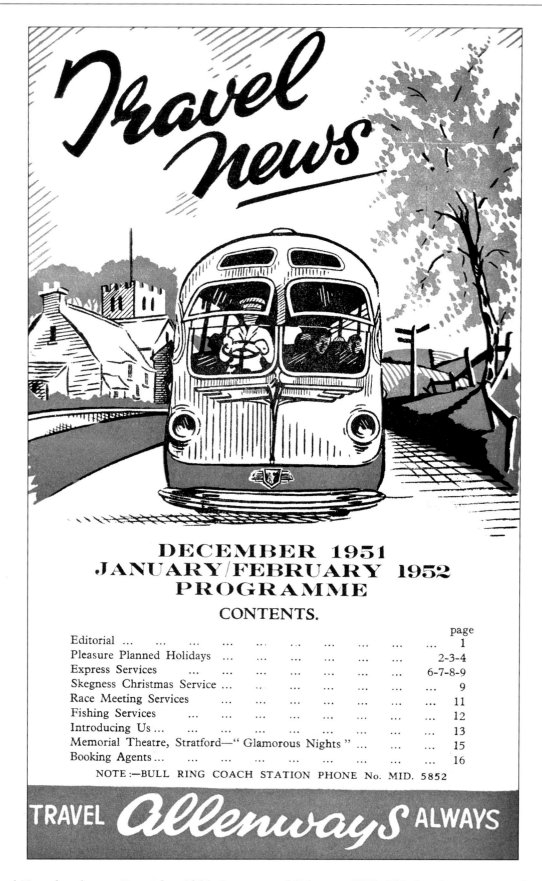

Travel News brochure - December 1951, January and February 1952. This brochure contained details of a Christmas service to Skegness as well as 1952 season Express Services, fishing excursions and race meeting trips. Some hotel inclusive breaks were also offered that were operated in conjunction with Wems Luxury Coaches of Weston-super-Mare.

"Introducing Us"....
In the 1950's editions of the company's "Travel News" brochures, a page was devoted to introduce members of the management, office and driving staff to the general public. A line drawing picture of each staff member together with a brief description of his or her character and duties was printed. Below are examples, with original descriptions, from 1951 and 1952.

SUPERINTENDENT REGINALD WEST. Mr West is responsible for the day-to-day control of traffic and vehicles. He is also in charge of the company's private hire department. He left the Midland "Red" in 1939 to join Allenways as a driver, being promoted to inspector in 1948 and to his present position in 1949.

INSPECTOR HARRY HAYNES. Happy by name and nature, has been driving for 36 years. As inspector in charge of the Eastern Division of the company's services, Inspector Haynes is responsible for the smooth operation of the company's largest service from Wolverhampton and Birmingham to Skegness. He joined the company in 1945 as a driver, was promoted to foreman driver in 1949 and in 1950 to the rank of Inspector.

MRS JOYCE CULL. Joyce is secretary to the traffic manager. Extremely efficient, she is one of the persons with whom the public seldom come in contact, but without whose efforts their travel would not be possible. Joyce has been with the company for some three years.

ERNEST NEVILLE CHAMBERLAIN. A Londoner aged 38, has had very vast experience as a coach driver, having driven for Greyhound Coaches in the United States and on the continent for Bartons. During the War he was Master-at-Arms on R.M.S. Queen Mary. Neville has a sparkling character which is reflected in his appearance.

LESLIE LEWIS, aged 27, a Londoner, is a fairly recent recruit to the Company's service, having joined us during the 1950 season. After serving 5½ years in the R.A.S.C., Leslie joined Geo. Ewer & Co. Ltd., of London, as driver on their well-known Grey Green Coaches. Leslie is an extremely good driver with the Londoner's amazing fund of good humour.

JACK HAMNET, aged 49, born in Birmingham, is a driver of very considerable experience, having had twenty years' as a driver of eight-wheel lorries before joining the company as a coach driver five years ago. He has been in the employ of the present management for about 15 years, Jack is in the front rank of his profession.

1951 - LOB 891, Leyland PSU1/15 Royal Tiger chassis with 37-seat Burlingham Seagull body. Named "Dollar Princess", this was one of three Burlingham bodied coaches purchased this year. The delivery of the first was featured in the Allenways "Travel News" Brochure - see below. Roy Marshall collection

As foreshadowed in last month's issue, at Whitsun the Dollar Princess and Princess Ida were placed in service, these two vehicles being the first of a series of new-type vehicles ordered by Allenways, utilising the new maximum dimensions authorised by the Ministry of Transport, namely 30 feet long by 8 feet wide. Based upon the Leyland Royal Tiger chassis, these vehicles have a 128 brake horsepower engine, placed horizontally under the centre of the coach, thus reducing noise to a minimum and avoiding all possibilities of fumes entering the saloon.

The coachwork, by Burlinghams of Blackpool, has extremely beautiful lines, as can be seen from the illustration. It is of all-metal construction, with extremely large windows giving maximum visability. Although seating four more passengers than the Castle Class Coaches, the majority of the additional length has been utilised to provide extra knee room. The increase in width has permitted the fitting of armchair reclining seating. Finally, the vehicles are equipped with a new type of underfloor heating, nine-valve H.M.V. Radio and fibre matting on the floor, folding tables in the rear of each seat.

Two new features of the Allenways Tour programme for June, published in this issue, are a combined coach and river tour to Evesham and Tewkesbury, full details of which are given in an article on page 6, and facilities for passengers on our tours to Rhyl to reserve their meals at the Alambra Cafe before leaving Birmingham, this reservation carries with it reduced admission charges to the Marine Lake Amusement Park. We feel that this will be of considerable help to our clients.

1951 - LOB 892, the second Burlingham Seagull bodied coach acquired this year. This was also built upon a Leyland Royal Tiger chassis and was given fleet number 23 and named "Princess Ida".
PM Photography

1951 - LOK 207, the third Burlingham Seagull, this time with an AEC Regal IV chassis. This coach was named "Princess Ena". These coaches were amongst the first in a new livery of grey and green.
RHG Simpson

JUNE PROGRAMME
(Festival of Britain, all centres see page 14)
TOURS FROM MAYPOLE — STIRCHLEY — MOSELEY ROAD — CITY

Friday, June 1st.

DAY TOUR — Aberystwyth	12/3
DAY TOUR — Rhyl	11/9
(Special facilities for meals and reduced admission to Marine Lake Amusement Park available)	
DAY TOUR — Thames Valley, including River Trip	15/-

Saturday, June 2nd.

EVENING TOUR — Henley-in-Arden and Alcester	3/6

Sunday, June 3rd.

DAY TOUR — Wicksteed Park	9/-
(The Children's Midland Paradise)	
DAY TOUR — New Brighton	14/6
DAY TOUR — Hampton Court	17/3
DAY TOUR — Weston-super-Mare	14/6
HALF-DAY TOUR — Compton Wynyates	8/6

Monday, June 4th.

DAY TOUR — Cheddar	12/3
DAY TOUR — Barry Island	12/3
DAY TOUR — Isle of Wight	17/6

Tuesday, June 5th.

DAY TOUR — Barmouth	12/3
DAY TOUR — Skegness	14/6
DAY TOUR — Wye Valley	11/9

Wednesday, June 6th.

DAY TOUR — Southampton	17/-
(Including Steamer Trip to see the "Queen Mary")	
DAY TOUR — Aberystwyth	12/3
DAY TOUR — Weston-super-Mare	12/3
HALF-DAY TOUR — Bourton-on-the-Water	6/6
EVENING TOUR — Henley and Alcester	3/6

Thursday, June 7th.

DAY TOUR — Burnham-on-Sea	12/3
DAY TOUR — Porthcawl	12/9
DAY TOUR — Dovedale	7/6

Friday, June 8th.

DAY TOUR — Barmouth	12/3
DAY TOUR — Weston-super-Mare	12/3
DAY TOUR — Wye Valley	11/9

Saturday, June 9th.

EVENING TOUR —	4/-
	14/6
	17/6
	20/6
	6/6

Samples of excursions available during 1951 and 1952.

Race Meetings
(All Tours leave from Station Street)

DECEMBER, 1951.

			Return	From
Saturday	1st	WORCESTER	5/9	11.45 a.m.
Monday	3rd	NOTTINGHAM	7/6	11.00 a.m.
Tuesday	4th	NOTTINGHAM	7/6	11.00 a.m.
Friday	7th	MANCHESTER	10/-	8.00 a.m
Saturday	8th	MANCHESTER	12/-	8.00 a.m.
Friday	14th	WARWICK	4/-	12.00 noon
Saturday	15th	WARWICK	4/9	12.00 noon
Wednesday	26th	WOLVERHAMPTON	4/-	11.00 a.m.
Thursday	27th	WOLVERHAMPTON	4/-	11.00 a.m.
Monday	31st	CHELTENHAM	7/-	10.30 a.m.

JANUARY, 1952.

Tuesday	1st	CHELTENHAM	7/-	10.30 a.m.
Tuesday	1st	MANCHESTER	10/-	8.00 a.m.
Wednesday	2nd	MANCHESTER	10/-	8.00 a.m.
Thursday	3rd	STRATFORD-ON-AVON	4/9	11.30 a.m.
Monday	7th	LEICESTER	6/6	11.00 a.m.
Tuesday	8th	LEICESTER	6/6	11.00 a.m.
Saturday	12th	WARWICK	4/9	12.00 noon
Monday	21st	NOTTINGHAM	7/6	11.00 a.m.
Tuesday	22nd	NOTTINGHAM	7/6	11.00 a.m.

FEBRUARY, 1952.

1st	MANCHESTER	10/-	8.00 a.m.
2nd	MANCHESTER	12/-	8.00 a.m.
4th	WARWICK	4/-	12.00 noon
5th	WARWICK	4/-	12.00 noon
11th	LEICESTER	6/6	11.00 a.m.
12th			
16th			
25th			
26th			
27th			
28th			

Festival of Britain
IMPORTANT FESTIVAL ATTRACTIONS
★

LONDON

May 4th/Sept. 30th — South Bank Exhibition.
1951 Exhibition of Books (Victoria & Albert Museum).
Exhibition of Architecture (Lansbury, Poplar).
Festival Pleasure Gardens, Battersea.
Exhibition of Science, South Kensington.
May 1st/Oct. 11th — Centenary of the Great Exhibition, 1851 (Victoria & Albert Museum).
May/June — Festival of the Arts—Theatreland en fête.

CHELTENHAM

July 2nd/14th — Festival of Contemporary Music.
Including Hallé Orchestra — London Symphony Orchestra — English Opera Group, etc., etc.

OXFORD

July 2nd/16th — Festival of the Arts.
Ashmolean Museum and Bodleian Library (Open to the Public).

WORCESTER

Aug. 30th/1st Sept. — Military Tattoo.
Sept. 2nd/7th — Three Choirs' Festival.
Also Exhibitions, Worcester Royal Porcelain Works Centenary.
Illuminated River Display, etc.

LLANGOLLEN

July 3rd/8th — International Eistedfodd.

STRATFORD-ON-AVON

Mar. 24th/October — Shakespeare Festival.
June 21st/23rd — Warwickshire and Oxford University.
Flower Show in conjunction with Natural Rose Society.
July 12th/14th — International Folk Dancing Festival.
July 28th (For 2 weeks)

ALLENWAYS FISHING SERVICES
EVERY SUNDAY
commencing
OCTOBER 7th, 1951
to

	Return
MONTFORD BRIDGE	
ATCHAM BRIDGE	6/6
BERRINGTON	5/3
COUND LODGE	5/3
FLADBURY	5/3
PERSHORE	4/9
DEFFORD	4/9
ECKINGTON	5/3
BREEDON	5/3
TWYNING FLEET	5/3
TEWKESBURY	5/9
LYDBROOK	7/-
ROSS	7/6
	7/-

Departing from:
BLAKE LANE, SMALL HEATH — 7.00 a.m.
BULL RING COACH STATION — 7.30 a.m.

Race Meetings and Fishing Trips were popular.
A wide range of trips celebrating "The Festival of Britain" was available during 1951.

1954 - A party of Birmingham Bookmakers, and their employees, pose for the camera before departing on a Sunday fishing excursion - a popular trip of the period. The picture was taken on Station Street in Birmingham where Allenways had their own departure stand. The driver, 21-year old Ron Steele, is on the far right. R Steele collection

TRAVEL *News*

1954

Weekly and Fortnightly

Express Services

to

Skegness	Boston
Pwllheli	Rhyl
Weston-S-Mare	Clevedon
Great Yarmouth	Lowestoft
Colwyn Bay	Llandudno

1954 edition of Allenways "Travel News" - this incorporated timetables and fares for the summer Express Coach Services.

CONDITIONS OF BOOKING

Baggage

All baggage carried free of charge at owner's risk. Passengers are allowed one normal suitcase per person. Push chairs, etc., cannot be carried without prior permission from the Company's Head Office.

Cancellations

All cancellations can only be dealt with by ALLENWAYS LTD., and not through Travel Agents, etc.

All the above and other conditions are published on the back of the ticket of travel to which intending passengers should refer.

OF INTEREST TO THE CHILDREN

Have you got your ALLENWAYS TRAVEL BADGE ?

This will be supplied free of charge upon application to ALLENWAYS LTD., 580 Moseley Road, Birmingham, 12, stating your travel ticket number and destination.

ALLENWAYS LIMITED

Head Office :
580 MOSELEY ROAD, BIRMINGHAM, 12
Telephone : CAL. 3191 and 3192

Coach Station :
BULL RING COACH STATION, PARK STREET, BIRMINGHAM
Telephone : MID. 3496 and 3497

Travel Allenways Always!

GUEST'S PRIORY PRESS, PRINTERS, 36, SUMMER HILL STREET, BIRMINGHAM

Have you got your Allenways Travel badge? These were available to children who travelled on the company's coach services.

1955 - ROG 209, Commer Avenger III chassis with 37-seat Burlingham Seagull body. Prior to entering service with Allenways, this coach was used by Commer as a demonstrator for a short period. It is pictured whilst taking part in the very first British Coach Rally, which was held at Clacton in April 1955. NA3T / ATPH

Another view of ROG 209 at the Coach Rally - the drivers are preparing the vehicle prior to it being judged in the "Concours d'Elegance". NA3T / ATPH

1956 edition of the Travel News brochure - this promoted Allenways own services to Boston, Wainfleet and Skegness, Pwllheli, Weston and Clevedon, Rhyl and Great Yarmouth. It also featured the services operated by Stockland Garage and Smiths Imperial Coaches - all of which could be booked at Allenways Booking office.

1956 - SOV 881, Commer Avenger III chassis with 41-seat Plaxton Venturer Mk II body - one of four identical coaches new this year. A Roberts collection

A nearside view of SOV 883, another Plaxton bodied Commer Avenger new for 1956.
RHG Simpson

1957 - TOV 268, the first of two new coaches for this year, a Commer Avenger III with Plaxton Venturer II 41-seat body. A Roberts collection

1957 - UOL 596, Commer Avenger IV chassis with 41-seat Plaxton Consort body. The Consort was Plaxton's new body for the 1957 season. A Roberts collection

1958 - VVP 541, Commer Avenger IV chassis with 41-seat Plaxton Consort II body - one of two new coaches for this year. RHG Simpson

VVP 542 was the second of the new Commer - Plaxtons delivered in 1958. The mark II version of the Plaxton Consort body was more pleasing than the previous version - the oval style front panel mouldings being favoured by many operators. Roy Marshall collection

1959 - No brand new coaches were added to the fleet this year but JOK 993 was a 1949 Maudslay Marathon 3 with 33-seat Plaxton body acquired from Palmer's of Birmingham. It joined the fleet in March but only spent a few months with Allenways as it was sold in December of the same year. PM Photography

1960 - 957 AOM, Ford Thames 570E chassis with 41-seat Duple Yeoman body. This combination of chassis and body was chosen for all new coaches purchased during the next few years. RHG Simpson

1960 - 959 AOM, another Ford Thames 570E with Duple Yeoman 41-seat body - five identical coaches were new to the fleet this year.

An offside view of another 1960 Duple bodied Ford Thames - 4462 VP. These coaches were painted in a new livery described as "Alpine Mauve and Mushroom". PM Photography

1960 Ford Thames - Duple, 4463 VP is pictured on the Moseley Road in Birmingham opposite Hawley's Bakery - a familiar sight for many years. Roy Marshall collection

1961 - 706 COM, one of four more Ford Thames 570E with 41-seat Duple Yeoman bodies. Note the change to the front windscreen design introduced by Duple for the 1961 season. A Roberts collection

1961 - Ford Thames - Duple Yeoman, 715 COM is pictured leaving the old Wembley Stadium whilst operating a private hire duty. RHG Simpson

A nearside view of 718 COM - another of the new coaches delivered in 1961. The Yeoman name was given to the body made by Duple on the Ford Thames chassis; it was basically the same as the Super Vega that was built on Bedford's SB series of chassis. A Roberts collection

1962 - 866 GOC was another Duple Yeoman bodied Ford Thames and the only new coach acquired this year. A red stripe was added to the livery on this vehicle - incorporated within the revised bright mouldings of the bodywork. Colin Ludford

1963 - KDD 345, a 1950 AEC Regal III chassis with 37-seat Plaxton body. This was one of a number of vehicles in the Allenways contract fleet. This separate fleet comprised entirely of used vehicles operated as "non PSV" and used mainly on contract to British Railways for maintenance staff transport. Jim Sheldon

1963 - 427 HOX, Ford Thames 570E chassis with 41-seat Duple Trooper body - one of three new this year. All three were painted in a darker shade of the "Alpine Mauve" livery - this particular coach was used for the first tour to Russia. Colin Ludford

A nearside view of 426 HOX, another 1963 Duple Trooper bodied Ford Thames. The Trooper body was part of a new range of bodies introduced by Duple for the 1963 season. Jim Sheldon

1963 - 648 JOC, Bedford VAL14 chassis with 52-seat Duple Vega Major body - the only example of this chassis and body type operated. Omnibus Society collection

1964 - PUX 74, Bedford SB8 chassis with 41-seat Duple Super Vega body - acquired from James, Liverpool in May of this year and operated for two years. The prefab building that served as the Booking Office at the Park Street Depot for many years can just be seen in this view. Colin Ludford

1964 - 140 LOC, Ford Thames 676E chassis with 52-seat Duple Marauder body pictured whilst in London. The Marauder body was later re-named "Mariner" by Duple. PM Photography

Another view of 140 LOC, pictured in the snow at the Park Street Depot. The site was next to the Moor Street Railway line and is now the new Moor Street multi-storey car park. Colin Ludford

1966 - FOA 766D, Ford R192 chassis with 45-seat Duple Empress body - pictured outside the Imperial Hotel in Ilfracombe. RHG Simpson

LWR 406, another vehicle from the contract fleet, a Bristol LS66 with 39-seat ECW body. This coach was new in 1952 to West Yorkshire and was acquired by Allenways in 1966. The Bristol - ECW combination proved favourable in the contract fleet with over 20 examples acquired in the late 1960's. Jim Sheldon

1966 - EVP 370D, Bedford VAL14 chassis with 52-seat Plaxton Panorama I body - one of two new for the fleet this year. Jim Sheldon

An offside view of EVP 370D, pictured whilst on hire to Flight's Coaches and in front of their depot on Berners Street in Lozells. Jim Sheldon

1969 - POB 819G, Ford R192 chassis with 41-seat Plaxton Panorama Elite body - one of three identical new coaches for this year. The Panorama Elite body was newly introduced by Plaxton for the 1969 season. Colin Ludford

POB 828G, another of the 1969 deliveries is pictured whilst operating an excursion to Southsea. Note the gold leaf lettering on the front nearside screen "Allenways New Executive Coach" - this was applied to the Plaxton bodied coaches acquired in the late 1960's and early 1970's. Omnibus Society collection

Allenways 1970
Express Coach Services

to

SKEGNESS * WESTON * CLEVEDON
PWLLHELI * GT. YARMOUTH
LOWESTOFT

ALLENWAYS LTD.
BULL RING COACH STATION AND BOOKING OFFICE
PARK STREET, BIRMINGHAM 5

Phone 021-643 7515

OR

BUTLIN'S GRAND PARADE
BULL RING CENTRE, BIRMINGHAM 5

Phone 021-643 8581

*

Also Agents for all leading Coach Operators with direct services

≡ *to* ≡

Ayr	Broadstairs	Exmouth	Lynmouth	Paignton	Sidmouth
Barry Island	Clacton	Filey	Lynton	Portsmouth	Southsea
Barmouth	Cliftonville	Ilfracombe	Margate	Ramsgate	Teignmouth
Blackpool	Colwyn Bay	Llandudno	Minehead	Rhyl	Tenby
Bognor Regis	Dawlish	Looe	Morecambe	Scarborough	Torquay
Bournemouth	Eastbourne	London	Newquay	Seaton	Weymouth

1970 leaflet for Express Coach Services.

43

1970 - TOX 139H, Ford R226 chassis with 52-seat Plaxton Panorama Elite body. Note in this view that "Shearings-Ribblesdale Pleasureways" fleet name is displayed on the glass side panel. This may have been removed from one of two ex Shearing group vehicles acquired in 1976 - the year that this coach left Allenways. Presumably the ex-Shearing coach received the panels lettered "Allenways". A Roberts collection

1971 / 1972 - Two new coaches were acquired in 1971 and three in 1972 - all were Ford R-series chassis with Plaxton Panorama Elite II bodies. Representing the 1971 duo is XOH 58J an R226 chassis with 49-seat body. Parked alongside is BOM 675K, which had the same chassis and body type but was fitted with 53 seats. John Mudge

FOC 101L was the fourth ex Superb Seddon. This coach was the only 12-metre Pennine VI version acquired and had 57 seats fitted in the Plaxton Panorama Elite II body. A Roberts collection

The oldest vehicles acquired with the Cantello businesses were three Bedford SB's with 41 - seat Duple Super Vega bodies. All three had been acquired by CF Cantello when Gee and Harrison of Whittington was taken over and were part of a batch of vehicles that were new to Jackson's Coaches of Castle Bromwich. 5422 NX represents these vehicles and is pictured when operating for Jackson's. RHG Simpson

CF Cantello acquired Darlaston based Mason's Coachways in 1969. The company was renamed "Masons - Superb" and the Superb Coaches' livery of gold, dark red and black was adopted. Caetano Lisboa bodied AEC Reliance, UON 10H was amongst the vehicles acquired by Allenways in 1973. John Mudge

Another ex Masons-Superb coach retained by Allenways was WOV 20J, it too was an AEC Reliance with 51-seat Caetano Lisboa body. Photobus

1974 - SOA 718M, Ford R1114 chassis with 53-seat Plaxton Panorama Elite III body - one of two new for the fleet this year. A Roberts collection

1974 brochure for Express Coach Services. All of the companies that now formed the Allenways group are listed on the front cover.

1974 - GOE 513N, Bedford VAS5 chassis with 29-seat Plaxton Panorama IV body. A similar coach, dating from 1972 was also acquired with the Superb Coaches' business in 1973. Omnibus Society collection

1975 - HAY 714L, Ford R226 chassis with 53-seat Plaxton Panorama Elite III body. Acquired from West, Woodford Green, this coach had the standard Elite III style of side body mouldings - all of the Elite III bodies acquired new by Allenways were fitted with the pattern of the previous Elite II as this was more suited to the fleet livery application. PM Photography

A small brochure published in the 1970's promoting all activities of the Allenways group. The apartments in Spain were owned by the Weatherhogg family but were occasionally made available for rent.

1975 - JOA 790N, Ford R1114 chassis with 53-seat Plaxton Elite III Express body - one of two new to the fleet this year. Andrew Roberts

JOA 791N was the second coach new in 1975 and this nearside view shows the twin driver-operated doors fitted to the "Express" version of Plaxton's Elite III body. Andrew Roberts

ALLENWAYS COACHES LIMITED

Allenways Private Hire Service

A large fleet of luxury coaches representing the best in modern transportation available for private or contract hire.

Our vehicles have:—

> Forced air ventilation.
> Radio.
> Public address system.
> Stereo tapes.
> First class heating.
> Large windows.
> Individual interior lights.
> Seating capacities of 12, 29, 41, 45, 49 & 53

Reservations made for:—

> Hotel accommodation.
> Theatres.
> Steamer trips.
> Catering.
> All special events.

Bookings made for:—

> Evening tours.
> Half day tours.
> Day tours.
> Extended British tours.
> Extended Overseas tours.

Allenways will attend to all your requirements and the company are backed by highly experienced staff with knowledge of all aspects of coach operation and planning.

TRAVEL ALLENWAYS – ALLWAYS

ALLENWAYS

LUXURY COACH EXPRESS SERVICES FOR

1976

DIRECT TO

SKEGNESS - WESTON - CLEVEDON
PWLLHELI - CRICCIETH - PORTMADOC
GREAT YARMOUTH - LOWESTOFT
COLWYN BAY - RHYL - LLANDUDNO

ALLENWAYS COACHES LTD.
10 FORTNUM CLOSE, BIRMINGHAM B33 0JT.
Tel; 021-784 4848

and

BUTLINS LTD. GRAND PARADE.
BULL RING CENTRE, BIRMINGHAM B5 4PF

Tel; 021- 643 8581

ALLENWAYS
GROUP

1976 Express Coach Services leaflet. The back page was used to promote the company's Private Hire Service.

1976 - MRY 720P, Ford R1114 chassis with 53-seat Plaxton Supreme body - one of six to join the fleet this year. Andrew Roberts

A nearside view of MRY 720P. The Supreme body was introduced in 1975 on short Bedford and Bristol chassis and then for the 1976 season for all 10, 11 and 12-metre vehicles. It was Plaxton's first all steel body and incorporated even larger side windows than the previous Elite series. Andrew Roberts

MRY 724P, another of the 1976 Plaxton Supreme bodied Fords. Four of the six left the fleet after only one season - MRY 720P and MRY 724P however remained with Allenways until 1986.
RHG Simpson

1978 - XMA 208M, a 1974 Ford R1114 with Plaxton Panorama Elite III 53-seat body - one of two acquired from the Shearings' group fleet. Andrew Roberts

1978 - VRY 728S, Ford R1114 chassis with 53-seat Plaxton Supreme body. Three similar coaches were purchased new this year and were the first examples of the revised "under floor engine" version of the Ford R-series chassis operated. Andrew Roberts

VRY 730S was another of the 1978 intake of coaches - all three incorporated "Bristol" type name domes over the front windscreen. This feature was specified for all future new Plaxton bodied coaches purchased by the company. RHG Simpson

ALLENWAYS

LUXURY COACH EXPRESS SERVICES FOR

1978

— DIRECT TO —

SKEGNESS - WESTON - CLEVEDON
PWLLHELI - CRICCIETH
PORTMADOC - LOWESTOFT
GREAT YARMOUTH

ALLENWAYS COACHES LIMITED
10 FORTNUM CLOSE, BIRMINGHAM B33 0JT.
Tel: 021-784 4848

BUTLINS LTD, GRAND PARADE
BULL RING CENTRE, BIRMINGHAM B5 4PF
Tel: 021-643 8581

TRAVEL ALLENWAYS
– ALLWAYS

ALLENWAYS GROUP

PWLLHELI, CRICCIETH, PORTMADOC

BIRMINGHAM to PWLLHELI
Saturday, 20th May to Saturday 16th September, 1978.
PWLLHELI to BIRMINGHAM
Saturday, 27th May to Saturday 23rd September, 1978.

Read down hrs.		Read up hrs.
07.30 dep.	BIRMINGHAM (7/9 Park Street) . . . . . . "	18.30
09.00 "	SHREWSBURY (Oak Hotel, Shrewsbury By-Pass) "	17.00
09.40 arr.	LLANGOLLEN . . . . .dep.	16.20
10.10 dep.	LLANGOLLEN . . . . arr.	15.50
12.00 arr.	PORTMADOC (Crosville Stand, High St.) . "	14.00
12.15 "	CRICCIETH (The Maes) . . . . "	13.45
12.30 "	PWLLHELI (Butlins Camp) . . . . "	13.30

FARE TABLE

BIRMINGHAM TO—	Return Fare Adults	Children
PWLLHELI	£8.65	£4.35
CRICCIETH	£8.45	£4.25
PORTMADOC.	£8.30	£4.15
SHREWSBURY TO—		
PWLLHELI	£6.50	£3.25
CRICCIETH	£6.35	£3.20
PORTMADOC.	£6.25	£3.15

WESTON and CLEVEDON

BIRMINGHAM to WESTON and CLEVEDON
Saturday, 27th May to Saturday, 26th August 1978.
WESTON & CLEVEDON to BIRMINGHAM
Saturday, 3rd June to Saturday, 2nd September 1978.

Read Down hrs.		Read up hrs.
08.30 dep.	BIRMINGHAM (7/9 Park Street)	arr. 15.15
08.40 "	BIRMINGHAM (580 Moseley Road)	" 15.05
09.00 "	RUBERY (Corporation Bus Terminus)	" 14.45
11.00 arr.	CLEVEDON (Binding & Payne Garages)	dep. 12.45
11.15 "	WESTON SUPER MARE (Locking Road Coach Park)	" 12.30

FARE TABLE

	Single		Return Fare	
	Ad.	Ch.	Ad.	Ch.
BIRMINGHAM TO WESTON SUPER MARE & CLEVEDON	£4.20	£2.10	£6.60	£3.30

GREAT YARMOUTH and LOWESTOFT

BIRMINGHAM to GREAT YARMOUTH and LOWESTOFT
Friday, 14th July to Friday 25th August, 1978.
GREAT YARMOUTH and LOWESTOFT to BIRMINGHAM
Saturday 22nd July to Saturday 2nd September, 1978.

Read down FRIDAYS hrs.		Read up SATURDAYS hrs.
23.55 dep.	BIRMINGHAM (7/9 Park Street)	arr. 22.05
SATURDAYS		
06.00 arr.	GT. YARMOUTH (Beach Coach Station)	dep. 16.00
06.30 "	LOWESTOFT (Battery Green Coach Station)	" 15.30

FARE TABLE

	Return Fare	
	Ad.	Ch.
BIRMINGHAM to— GT. YARMOUTH & LOWESTOFT	£9.60	£4.80

1978 Express Coach Service leaflet and time-tables for the North Wales, Weston and Great Yarmouth routes. Note that the service to Great Yarmouth was operated over-night on Fridays.

1979 - GEA 706T, Ford R1114 chassis with 53-seat Plaxton Supreme IV body - one of three new this year. The livery on these coaches was revised to incorporate a red stripe that extended from the front indicator housing - the design was based upon Plaxton's show coaches and demonstrators for the Mk IV Supreme body. Andrew Roberts

A nearside view of GEA 706T - note that the red stripe was not complete in this view, the coach was delivered painted in this manner and was operated for some months before the livery was modified. Andrew Roberts

FFK 668T, another 1979 Plaxton Supreme IV bodied Ford R1114. Note the slight differences in the application of the livery compared to GEA 706T on the previous page. PM Photography

1979 - PDM 43P, one of two 1976 Ford R1114 chassis with 53-seat Plaxton Supreme bodies acquired from Shearings this year. PM Photography

Several members of the fleet had their livery updated with a red stripe to match the Plaxton Supreme IV bodied coaches - as depicted here in this view of MRY 724P. A Roberts collection

VRY 728S also received large "Allenways" fleet name towards the back of the body in addition to the red stripe. Andrew Roberts

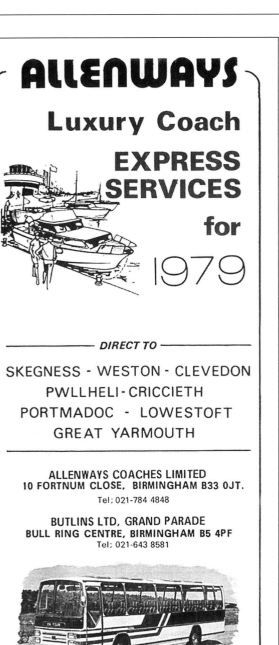

1979 and 1980 editions of the Express Coaches leaflet.

1980 - Three more Plaxton bodied Ford R1114s were added to the fleet including LUE 240V which had the Express version of the Supreme IV body. Andrew Roberts

LUE 244V, another of the 1980 Ford - Plaxtons - this coach was fitted with a coach style door. Although basically similar, there were slight differences to the livery application of the coaches purchased between 1979 and 1982. Andrew Roberts

1981 - UBC 464X, Volvo B10M 12-metre chassis with 51-seat Plaxton Supreme V GT body. This was the first Volvo purchased by the company. R Steele

An offside view of UBC 464X - the "GT" version of the Plaxton Supreme body included many items as standard that were only usually available at extra cost. These included Plaxton's "relaxa" reclining seats with arm rests, tinted windows, full-draw curtains, wheel trims and a chrome front grill. R Steele

1982 - VAY 222X, Ford R1114 chassis with 51-seat Plaxton Supreme V GT body. This and similar coach, UBC 644X, were that last Fords purchased. Andrew Roberts

VAY 222X and GEA 706T pictured at the Fortnum Close, Tile Cross depot. Andrew Roberts

1984 - The last coaches purchased by Allenways under the ownership of the Weatherhogg family were A370 UNH and A380 UNH, two Volvo B10M chassis with Jonckheere Jubilee P50 bodies. Both seated 49 passengers in reclining seats and had an on-board toilet and video equipment. They were painted in a simple livery of silver with mauve lower skirt panels and the fleet name applied in black lettering. A Roberts collection

A380 UNH is pictured with signs fitted for Walsall based tour operator Hoverland. Both coaches were deployed on tours to Austria, and occasionally Spain, for this company. RHG Simpson

Long serving Allenways driver, Ron Steele, is pictured with A380 UNH when new at Aston Hall in Birmingham. A Roberts collection

After the Weatherhogg family ceased operations in 1986, the Allenways name passed to David Watkins who also operated Claribel Coaches. D525 BBV, a Duple 425 integral was acquired in 1987 and operated with Allenways fleet name in silver based livery with red stripes. R Steele

D525 BBV had been used for a short time by Duple as a demonstrator. The 425 gained its name because of the designs aerodynamic drag factor of 0.425. It was and integral vehicle with a stainless steel frame and Cummins running gear - although a DAF engine option was also available. R Steele

A second Duple 425, F32 KHS, was acquired in 1989. The coach is pictured here whilst operating a tour of the French Battlefields. R Steele

A rear view of F32 KHS - the Allenways fleet name was prominently displayed on the rear panel. R Steele

BIRMINGHAM TO RUSSIA
- WITH ALLENWAYS

Allenways' coaches were no strangers to continental travel. The company's vehicles were sent to most parts of Western Europe whilst working for Schools groups and Tour Operators.

One of the most unusual journeys undertaken by the company was a regular tour of the former Soviet Union. The 2,500-mile journey took in five European capitals and passed through Belgium, Western Germany, Austria, Hungary, and Romania to the Black Sea resort of Odessa.

Once at Odessa passengers had the choice of either taking a flight to Moscow, and then train to Kiev, or stay in Odessa and then travel to Kiev in the coach for the return journey which was made through the former country of Czechoslovakia. Five nights were spent in Odessa and four in Kiev. The outward journey took eight days and travelled via Vienna, Gyor in Hungary, Budapest, Oradea, Trigu Maures and Lasi in Romania. The return journey was a day less and went via Lvov in Russia, Presov, Brno and Prague in Czechoslovakia.

These tours were undertaken on behalf of local schoolmaster, Alan Chambers, with Allenways' foreman driver Ron Steele driving. The first departure was in 1963 in a 41-seat Duple Trooper bodied Ford Thames. This pioneer departure was followed by two or three tours each year up to 1991. The tours were aimed primarily at schoolchildren with accommodation arranged at Youth Hostels and Camp Sites. A similar tour was occasionally operated to Istanbul.

Today it seems surprising that most of these tours were operated by "lightweight" coaches, but the Ford based vehicles coped well with the arduous journey. There were some incidents of course, one notable one being in 1973 when, fortunately, three coaches were operating a departure. One of the coaches broke down about 200 miles from Odessa and it was diagnosed that a piston had broken through the engine block. The vehicle was towed to a garage in Kishinev and one of the other coaches that had already arrived in Odessa, was sent to pick-up the stranded group. Back in the UK, Allenways' General Manager, Ray Taylor, and another driver, hastily arranged Visas and other paperwork in preparation for the 2,000 plus mile journey with a replacement engine. The coach was repaired in time for the group to continue their journey after the scheduled break in Odessa.

Ron Steele's 52nd, and last, trip in 1991 would however prove to be rather more memorable than most. The Watkiss family had by this time taken-over the Allenways name and sent one of their Duple 425 integrals. The coach was travelling through a violent storm along the road from Romania to Kischinev and had to stop behind other stationary vehicles. Unfortunately the car following had defective brakes and collided with the coach. The car driver was rushed to hospital but unfortunately died. The coach was taken to Sovinteravto Service in Kischinev for repairs and was later taken to Odessa by an emergency driver. Next followed a six-week nightmare for Ron, whose passport had been confiscated pending an inquiry into the accident by the local police. A debate about the validity of the insurance for the coach led to lots of wrangling and interviews but it was finally agreed that compensation should be paid to the car driver's family - even though the accident was his fault. A campaign to help Ron had been started back in Birmingham and eventually, after donations from friends, Birmingham coach drivers and past customers, a transfer of cash to a Russian Bank was arranged in order for Ron to be set free.

One of the Duple 425s operated by the Watkiss family is pictured in Kiev during one of the last Russian tours operated by Allenways. R Steele

Allenways - Fleet list

	Reg.	Chassis	Body	Seats	New	Acquired	Sold	Note
	OX 6032	Leyland PLC1	Buckingham	C26R	1928	3/28	1949	
8	VP 9140	Leyland LTB1	Buckingham	C26R	1929	5/29	1949	
	VP 9141	" "	"	C26R	1929	5/29	1949	
4	VP 9142	" "	"	C26R	1929	5/29	1949	
3	VP 9143	" "	"	C26R	1929	6/29	1947	
7	AOF 191	Leyland TS6	Burlingham	C32R	1934	7/34	12/53	
	AG 4503	AEC Reliance	Mains	C32R	1929	1935	5/41	Ex Western SMT
8	BOX 499	Maudslay SF40	Burlingham	C32F	1936	4/36	7/54	"Colchester Castle"
6	HE 5994	Daimler CP6	Brush	C28F	1933	?	3/51	Ex Yorkshire Traction 371
7	HE 5995	" "	"	C28F	1933	?	10/49	Ex Yorkshire Traction 372
9	FON 849	Bedford OWB	Mulliner	B32F	1943	3/43	7/47	
10	DON 246	Leyland SKPZ2	Burlingham	C26F	1937	1944	2/51	Ex Sugden, Birmingham
9	COV 592	Maudslay ML5	Auto-Cellulose	C32F	1937	7/47	?	Ex Cave, Birmingham
11	HON 401	Leyland SKPZ2	Burlingham	C27R	1948	3/48	4/53	
14	JOH 155	Leyland TS2	N.M.U.	C33F	1948	12/48	7/53	Ex Noakes, Pensnett
12	FR 9649	Leyland TS1	N.M.U.	C33F	1928	3/49	?	Ex Chinn, Shirley "Cardiff Castle"
17	JOK 367	Commer Commando	Plaxton	C30F	1949	3/49	4/50	
18	JOH 880	Guy Arab III 6DC	Barnard	C33F	1949	3/49	4/55	"Warwick Castle"
19	JOH 881	" " " "	"	C33F	1949	4/49	12/55	
20	JOH 882	" " " "	"	C33F	1949	6/49	4/55	"Nottingham Castle"
21	JOH 883	" " " "	"	C33F	1949	7/49	12/55	
22	GTF 113	Guy Arab III 5LW	Santus	C33F	1947	6/49	9/55	Ex Roberts, Crewe
23	KOC 662	Foden PVF6	Lincs Trailer	HDC43F	1950	6/50	12/53	"City of Birmingham"
24	KOC 663	" "	" "	" "	1950	6/50	7/58	"City of Lincoln"
25	KOC 664	Leyland CP01	Plaxton	C28F	1950	3/50	4/58	
26	KOC 665	Commer Avenger 1	Plaxton	C33F	1950	2/50	11/56	"Windsor Castle"
28	LOB 891	Leyland PSU1/15	Burlingham Seagull	C37C	1951	5/51	1/56	"Dollar Princess"
29	LOB 892	" "	" "	C37C	1951	5/51	12/55	"Princess Ida"
32	LOK 207	AEC Regal IV	Burlingham Seagull	C37C	1951	7/51	1/56	"Princess Ena"
33	EAY 985	Maudslay Marathon 2	Duple	C35F	1948	5/52	11/57	Ex Brown, Sapcote
34	KOC 527	Commer Avenger 1	Plaxton	C33F	1949	1952	11/56	Ex P Payne, Birmingham
	UMP 231	Austin CXB	Whitson	C29F	1949	1/54	12/55	Ex Marsden, Aldershot
	ROG 209	Commer Avenger III	Burlingham Seagull	C37F	1955	3/55	3/59	
	EBA 264	Commer Avenger I	Plaxton	C32F	1949	6/55	2/60	Ex Watson, Selby
	KNF 156	" " "	"	C33F	1950	1955	10/57	Originally Shearing, Oldham
	FNR 419	" " "	"	C33F	1949	7/55	10/56	Ex Hutchinson, Middleton
	SOV 880	Commer Avenger III	Plaxton Venturer II	C41F	1956	2/56	2/60	
	SOV 881	" " "	" " "	C41F	1956	3/56	11/59	
	SOV 882	" " "	" " "	C41F	1956	3/56	2/60	
	SOV 883	" " "	" " "	C41F	1956	3/56	2/60	
	TOV 268	" " "	" " "	C41F	1957	1957	11/60	
	UOL 596	Commer Avenger IV	Plaxton Consort	C41F	1957	5/57	2/61	
	VVP 541	Commer Avenger IV	Plaxton Consort II	C41F	1958	3/58	2/61	
	VVP 542	" " "	" " "	C41F	1958	3/58	11/60	
	JOK 993	Maudslay Marathon 3	Plaxton	C33F	1949	3/59	12/59	Ex Palmer, Birmingham
	957 AOM	Ford Thames 570E	Duple Yeoman	C41F	1960	2/60	10/62	
	958 AOM	" " "	" "	C41F	1960	2/60	11/61	
	959 AOM	" " "	" "	C41F	1960	2/60	11/61	
	4462 VP	" " "	" "	C41F	1960	2/60	1/63	
	4463 VP	" " "	" "	C41F	1960	2/60	1/66	
	706 COM	" " "	" "	C41F	1961	2/61	1/65	
	715 COM	" " "	" "	C41F	1961	2/61	11/62	
	716 COM	" " "	" "	C41F	1961	2/61	1/66	
	718 COM	" " "	" "	C41F	1961	2/61	1/64	
	JX 3894	Leyland TS7	Burlingham	C32F	1936	7/61	12/61	Ex Superb, Birmingham
	DUH 876	Daimler CVD6	Harrington	C33F	1948	8/61	7/63	Ex Morris, Pencoed
	448 EOP	Ford Thames 570E	Duple Yeoman	C41F	1961	11/61	1/65	
	KNP 609	Bedford SB8	Plaxton	C33F	1951	1/62	10/63	Ex Hayes, Lye
	NOF 950	Bedford SB8	Duple Vega	C33F	1953	4/62	10/63	Ex Bates, Birmingham
	MKV 2	Bedford SB8	Plaxton	C35F	1953	5/62	4/64	Ex Chivers, Midsomer Norton
	866 GOC	Ford Thames 570E	Duple Yeoman	C41F	1962	6/62	1/66	
	793 ART	Commer Avenger IV	Yeates	C41F	1959	9/62	4/63	Ex Lee, Stapleford
	NOF 343	AEC Regal IV	Plaxton	C41C	1953	12/62	5/63	Ex Birmingham Co-op
	425 HOX	Ford Thames 570E	Duple Trooper	C41F	1963	4/63	12/66	
	426 HOX	" " "	" "	C41F	1963	3/63	12/66	

Reg.	Chassis	Body	Seats	New	Acquired	Sold	Note
427 HOX	Ford Thames 570E	Duple Trooper	C41F	1963	3/63	4/66	
648 JOC	Bedford VAL14	Duple Vega Major	C52F	1963	4/63	11/67	
LAO 646	Leyland PSU1/15	Burlingham Seagull	C37C	1952	6/63	11/63	Ex Dickson, Stoke Mandeville
140 LOC	Ford Thames 676E	Duple Marauder	C52F	1964	3/64	11/66	
PUX 74	Bedford SB8	Duple Vega	C41F	1958	5/64	5/66	Ex James, Liverpool
343 MOP	Ford Thames 570E	Duple Trooper	C41F	1964	6/64	10/68	
587 KRE	Commer Avenger III	Duple	C41F	1956	7/64	3/65	Ex Mason, Darlaston
KNY 625	Leyland PS1/1	Burlingham	FC33F	1950	10/64	5/65	Ex Morgan & Evans, Cwmllynfell
AOL 823B	Ford Thames 570E	Duple Trooper	C41F	1964	12/64	10/67	
BOF 167C	" " "	" "	C41F	1965	1/65	1/69	
BOF 168C	" " "	" "	C41F	1965	1/65	4/69	
BOK 912C	" " "	" "	C41F	1965	4/65	4/69	
COX 400C	Bedford SB5	Duple Bella Vega	C41F	1965	6/65	4/66	
WKO 136	Beadle-Commer	Beadle	C41C	1956	7/65	4/66	Ex Bown, Birmingham
MFM 697	Bristol LWL6B	ECW	FC35F	1951	2/66	9/66	Ex Crosville CLB 266
EVP 369D	Bedford VAL14	Plaxton Panorama I	C52F	1966	3/66	12/69	
EVP 370D	" " "	" " "	C52F	1966	3/66	3/70	
FOA 766D	Ford R192	Duple Empress	C45F	1966	5/66	1/72	
LWR 406	Bristol LS6G	ECW	C39F	1952	5/66	7/69	Ex West Yorkshire CUG 1
HBL 74	" "	"	C39F	1952	8/66	6/67	Ex South Midland 672
KNG 706	Bristol LWL6B	ECW	FC35F	1951	2/67	2/68	Ex Eastern Counties LS706
HOV 223E	Ford R192	Plaxton Panorama I	C41F	1967	3/67	1/72	
HOV 224E	Bedford VAL14	Plaxton Panorama I	C52F	1967	2/67	4/71	
LTA 999	Bristol LS6G	ECW	C39F	1953	3/67	3/68	Ex Southern National 1343
LOK 445F	Ford R226	Duple Viceroy	C52F	1968	1/68	1/72	
ECN 689	Guy Arab LUF6HLW	Weyman	C37F	1955	4/68	2/69	Ex Northern General 1689
6299 WE	AEC Reliance 2MURV	Plaxton Panorama	C41F	1959	11/68	5/69	Ex Sheffield United 299
POB 819G	Ford R192	Plaxton Panorama Elite	C41F	1969	2/69	4/80	
POB 827G	" "	" " "	C41F	1969	4/69	5/79	
POB 828G	" "	" " "	C41F	1969	4/69	4/79	
XTA 846	Beadle-Commer	Beadle	C41F	1957	4/69	?	Ex Hesaltine, Featherstone
WAT 675	Leyland PSUC1/2	Harrington	C35F	1957	5/69	12/70	Ex East Yorkshire 675
WAT 676	" " "	"	C35F	1957	5/69	12/70	" " " 676
WAT 677	" " "	"	C35F	1957	5/69	12/70	" " " 677
TOX 139H	Ford R226	Plaxton Panorama Elite	C52F	1970	3/70	3/76	
TOX 140H	" "	" " "	C52F	1970	3/70	2/76	
XOH 57J	Ford R192	Plaxton Panorama Elite II	C41F	1971	4/71	3/80	
XOH 58J	Ford R226	Plaxton Panorama Elite II	C49F	1971	4/71	6/78	
BOM 673K	" "	" " "	C53F	1972	1/72	10/76	
BOM 674K	" "	" " "	C49F	1972	1/72	4/78	
BOM 675K	" "	" " "	C53F	1972	1/72	6/74	
NUK 558K	Ford Transit	Deansgate	12	1972	6/73	3/77	Ex Dolan, Newport
JOH 208L	Bedford YRT	Plaxton Panorama Elite III	C53F	1973	7/73	3/77	
SOA 718M	Ford R1114	Plaxton Panorama Elite III	C53F	1974	6/74	1984	
SOA 719M	" "	Plaxton Elite Express III	C53F	1974	6/74	7/80	
GOE 513N	Bedford VAS5	Plaxton Panorama IV	C29F	1974	10/74	2/78	
5422 NX	Bedford SB1	Duple Super Vega	C41F	1960	2/75	12/75	Ex Superb, Birmingham
5423 NX	" "	" " "	C41F	1960	2/75	12/75	" " "
9259 UE	" "	" " "	C41F	1961	2/75	12/75	" " "
ERF 3 B	Bedford SB5	Duple Bella Vega	C41F	1964	2/75	4/76	" " "
CON 782C	AEC Reliance 2MU3RA	Plaxton Panorama I	C45F	1965	2/75	8/75	" " "
NOG 882F	AEC Reliance 6U3ZR	Plaxton Panorama I	C53F	1968	2/75	4/76	" " "
NOG 883F	" " "	" " "	C53F	1968	2/75	8/76	" " "
XOC 103J	Bedford YRQ	Duple Viceroy	C45F	1971	2/75	2/76	" " "
XOC 104J	" "	" "	C45F	1971	2/75	12/75	" " "
XOL 105J	" "	" "	C45F	1971	2/75	12/75	" " "
XOL 300J	" "	" "	C45F	1971	2/75	12/75	" " "
XON 400J	" "	" "	C45F	1971	2/75	12/75	" " "
XOV 500J	" "	" "	C45F	1971	2/75	4/76	" " "
BOP 106K	Seddon Pennine IV	Plaxton Panorama Elite II	C53F	1972	2/75	12/75	" " "
COX 600K	" " "	" " " "	C53F	1972	2/75	12/75	" " "
COX 900K	Seddon Pennine IV	Duple Viceroy	C53F	1972	2/75	8/75	" " "
FOC 101L	Seddon Pennine VI	Plaxton Panorama Elite II	C57F	1972	2/75	8/75	" " "
FOC 800L	Bedford VAS5	Plaxton Panorama IV	C29F	1972	2/75	5/78	" " "
FOL 100L	Bedford YRT	Plaxton Elite Express III	C53F	1972	2/75	3/77	" " "
MDH 307E	Bedford VAM	Duple Viceroy	C45F	1967	2/75	3/78	Ex Mason, Darlaston
HAY 714L	Ford R226	Plaxton Panorama Elite III	C53F	1973	6/75	9/79	Ex West, Woodford Green
JOA 790N	Ford R1114	Plaxton Elite Express III	C53F	1975	7/75	1/86	

Reg.	Chassis	Body	Seats	New	Acquired	Sold	Note
JOA 791N	Ford R1114	Plaxton Elite Express III	C53F	1975	7/75	8/85	
NTU 173L	Ford R226	Plaxton Panorama Elite III	C53F	1973	2/76	7/79	Ex Batty Holt, Altrincham
NTU 182L	Ford R226	Plaxton Panorama Elite III	C53F	1973	2/76	1/80	Ex Pleasureways, Altrincham
MRY 719P	Ford R1114	Plaxton Supreme	C53F	1976	4/76	5/77	
MRY 720P	" "	" "	C53F	1976	4/76	4/86	
MRY 721P	" "	" "	C53F	1976	4/76	5/77	
MRY 722P	" "	" "	C53F	1976	4/76	5/77	
MRY 723P	" "	" "	C53F	1976	4/76	5/77	
MRY 724P	" "	" "	C53F	1976	4/76	1/86	
XMA 207M	Ford R1114	Plaxton Panorama Elite III	C53F	1974	12/77	6/84	Ex Shearing, Altrincham
XMA 208M	" "	" " " "	C53F	1974	1/78	9/82	" " "
VRY 728S	Ford R1114	Plaxton Supreme	C53F	1978	3/78	6/84	
VRY 730S	" "	" "	C53F	1978	4/78	5/84	
VRY 732S	Ford R1114	Plaxton Supreme Express	C53F	1978	6/78	12/84	
PDM 43P	Ford R1114	Plaxton Supreme	C53F	1976	3/79	1/86	Ex Shearing, Altrincham
NNF 161P	" "	" "	C53F	1976	3/79	3/82	" " "
FFK 668T	Ford R1114	Plaxton Supreme IV	C53F	1979	4/79	6/86	
GEA 706T	" "	" " "	C53F	1979	7/79	1/86	
GEA 708T	" "	" " "	C53F	1979	7/99	1986	
LUE 240V	Ford R1114	Plaxton Supreme IV Express	C53F	1980	3/80	1/86	
LUE 242V	Ford R1114	Plaxton Supreme IV	C53F	1980	3/80	5/86	
LUE 244V	" "	" " "	C53F	1980	4/80	2/86	
UBC 464X	Volvo B10M	Plaxton Supreme V GT	C51F	1981	12/81	3/86	
UBC 644X	Ford R1114	Plaxton Supreme V GT	C51F	1982	2/82	12/85	
VAY 222X	" "	" " "	C51F	1982	2/82	9/86	
PUT 157W	Volvo B58	Duple Dominant II	C50FT	1981	2/82	2/86	Ex Anthony, Liverpool
A370 UNH	Volvo B10M	Jonckheere Jubilee P50	C49FT	1984	4/84	4/86	
A380 UNH	" "	" " "	C49FT	1984	3/84	4/86	

NOTES

OX 6032	Was re-bodied FC ? F in 1936 and later re-numbered 6
AOF 191	Was re-bodied by Allenways as C33F in 1949 and re-numbered 15
BOX 499	Was extensively re-built by Allenways as C33F in 1950
HE 5994 / 5	Were re-bodied by Harrington as C32F - the origin of these bodied is unknown, but they were second-hand
HON 401	Was re-registered (original number not known). The Burlingham body was new in 1938
FR 9649	The body of this coach was new in 1946
JOH 155	Was re-registered from TY 4495 and re-bodied prior to going into service with Allenways.
JOH 881	Was re-bodied by Yeates in 1952 as FC37F
JX 3894	Was re-bodied in 1950 by a previous owner

ALLENWAYS CONTRACT FLEET

Reg.	Chassis	Body	Seats	New	Acquired	Sold	Note
JX 3894	Leyland TS7	Burlingham	C32F	1936	12/61	12/61	Ex Allenways PSV fleet
DUH 876	Daimler CVD6	Harrington	C33F	1948	7/63	?	" " " "
KNP 609	Bedford SB	Plaxton	C33F	1951	10/63	?	" " " "
NOF 950	Bedford SB	Duple	C35F	1953	10/63	?	" " " "
KDD 345	AEC Regal III	Plaxton	FC37F	1950	10/63	?	Ex G P Smith, Bristol
OUB 28	Crossley SD42/9	Yeates	C37F	1951	10/63	?	Ex Granville, Grimsby
LTC 721	Maudslay Marathon 3	Duple	FC33F	1950	1964	?	Ex Jennings, Ipswich
MUY 141	Bedford SBO	Plaxton	C38F	1954	1964	11/69	Ex Olds, Birmingham
MKV 2	Bedford SB	Plaxton	C35F	1953	4/64	3/66	Ex Allenways PSV fleet
963 CRE	Leyland PSUC1/2	Duple	C41C	1954	1964	2/68	Ex Greatrex, Stafford
KFD 554	Leyland PS1/1	Burlingham	C33F	1950	7/64	?	Ex Hill, Tredegar
DTH 819	Leyland PS1/1	Burlingham	FC37F	1949	1965	12/66	Ex Noakes, Pensnett
MMB 768	" "	"	FC37F	1949	1/66	12/66	" " "
KNY 625	Leyland PS1/1	Burlingham	FC33F	1950	1966	?	Ex Harper, Birmingham
LTA 965	Bristol LWL6B	ECW	FC37F	1951	3/66	11/68	Ex Southern National 1331
WKO 136	Commer-Beadle	Beadle	C41C	1956	4/66	9/67	Ex Allenways PSV fleet
LTA 763	Bristol LWL6B	ECW	FC37F	1951	5/66	4/68	Ex Western National 1318
LWR 409	Bristol LS6G	ECW	C39F	1952	5/66	7/69	Ex West Yorkshire CUG 4
MFM 697	Bristol LWL6B	ECW	FC35F	1951	9/66	6/68	Ex Allenways PSV fleet
LTA 929	Bristol LWL6B	ECW	FC37F	1951	10/66	4/68	Ex Southern National 1333

Reg.	Chassis	Body	Seats	New	Acquired	Sold	Note
LTA 964	Bristol LWL6B	ECW	FC37F	1951	10/66	4/68	Ex Southern National 1330
PHW 950	Bristol LS6B	ECW	C39F	1953	12/66	5/69	Ex Rodgers, Redcar
HBL 74	Bristol LS6G	ECW	C39F	1952	6/67	11/68	Ex Allenways PSV fleet
OTE 72	Guy Arab IV 6LW	NCME	H31/26R	1952	1/68	?	Ex Lancashire United 489
ECN 685	Guy Arab LUF 6HLW	Weyman	C37F	1955	2/68	?	Ex Northern General 1685
SHN 717	Bristol LS6B	ECW	C38F	1953	4/68	2/71	Ex United UT 2
SHN 720	" "	"	C38F	1953	4/68	?	Ex United UT 5
UHN 344	" "	"	C38F	1954	4/68	2/70	Ex United UT 8
UHN 345	" "	"	C38F	1954	4/68	2/70	Ex United UT 9
SHN 716	" "	"	C38F	1953	6/68	2/70	Ex United UT 1
UHN 349	" "	"	C38F	1954	6/68	?	Ex United UT 13
LHE 503	Leyland PSUC1/2T	Burlingham	C41F	1957	11/68	5/69	Ex Yorkshire Traction 101
ECN 689	Guy Arab LUF6HLW	Weyman	C37F	1955	2/69	1/70	Ex Northern General 1685
OTT 39	Bristol LS6G	ECW	C41F	1953	5/69	?	Ex Western National 1357
6299 WE	AEC Reliance 2MU3RV	Plaxton	C41F	1959	5/69	9/70	Ex Allenways PSV fleet
XDV 859	AEC Reliance MU3RV	Willowbrook	C41F	1958	6/69	1/71	Ex Greenslades, Exeter
LTA 878	Bristol LS6G	ECW	C41F	1953	7/69	1/70	Ex Western National 1350
OTT 38	" "	"	C41F	1953	7/69	1/71	Ex Western National 1356
OTT 71	" "	"	C41F	1953	7/69	1/70	Ex Southern National 1362
OTT 72	" "	"	C41F	1953	7/69	?	Ex Southern National 1363
OTT 87	" "	"	C41F	1953	7/69	?	Ex Southern National 1378
LTA 872	" "	"	C41F	1952	8/69	12/69	Ex Western National 1344
OTT 78	" "	"	C41F	1953	8/69	8/70	Ex Southern National 1369

NOTE

DTH 819 and MMB 768 were re-bodied in the 1950's with Seagull style bodies

---

COACHES OWNED BY CLARIBEL COACHES AND LICENSED TO ALLENWAYS

(All were in Claribel / Birmingham International livery - except D525 BBV and F 32 KHS which had Allenways fleetnames)

Reg.	Chassis	Body	Seats	New	Acquired	Sold	Note
D525 BBV	Hestair-Duple	Duple 425	C53FT	1987	6/87	4/92	
MAW 112P	Ford R1114	Plaxton Supreme	C49F	1976	9/87	1991	Ex Claribel, Birmingham
E 52 TYG	Leyland Royal Tiger	Leyland Doyen	C53FT	1988	4/89	3/91	Ex West Riding 52
E 53 TYG	" " "	" "	C53FT	1988	4/89	8/92	" " " 53
WWA 299Y	Leyland Tiger	Plaxton Paramount 3500	C53F	1983	4/89	8/92	" " " 54
F 32 KHS	Hestair-Duple	Duple 425	C53F	1989	6/89	8/92	
YGY 638Y	Leyland Tiger	Plaxton Paramount 3500	C50F	1983	4/89	8/92	Ex Yorkshire Woollen 62
D497 YMO	Renault-Dodge	Howells	C16F	1987	6/89	8/91	Ex Howell, Deri
G155 XJF	Toyota Coaster	Caetano Optimo	C21F	1990	3/90	8/92	
G234 YVL	Volvo B10M	Jonckheere Deauville	C51FT	1990	5/90	4/92	

Radley Motors, Superb Coaches and Mason's Coachways

Mr Frank C Cantello - known as Cecil by family and friends had worked for many years as a driver for Jackson's Coaches of Castle Bromwich. In 1956 he obtained his own coach, a 1950 Albion with 33-seat Bellhouse Hartwell body and started operating as "Radley Motors".

The coach was garaged in Cooks Lane, Kitts Green and serviced by a neighbouring garage. The business grew quickly and a wide variety of vehicle makes found their way into the fleet including Leyland, Guy, Bedford, Foden and Daimler.

In 1960 Dennis Cantello, brother of CF Cantello joined the business, and in the same year, the first brand new coaches were also acquired when two Duple Yeoman bodied Ford Thames were purchased. The fleet moved to another base at 193 Mackadown Lane, Tile Cross and in 1964 control of Superb Coaches (Birmingham) Limited was obtained.

The origins of Superb Coaches go back to March 1951 when S Small started to trade as "Superb Coaches" from 47 South Road, Birmingham 11. In February 1952 H Parker and H Etherton joined him and the company moved to Eachelhurst Road in Pype Hayes. At about the same time some licences were also obtained from Heathcote and Llewellyn Limited including a seasonal service to Margate.

A limited company "Superb Coaches (Birmingham) Limited" was formed to take-over the business and in 1955 the share capital of Ideal Coaches (Birmingham) Limited was also acquired. Before being acquired by CF Cantello, the operation moved two more times, first to 289 Yardley Green Road in Bordesley Green and then, in 1964, to Blake Lane. Mostly second-hand vehicles were operated including many double-decker buses, although a number of brand-new coaches were obtained in the early 1960's - these were painted in a livery of black and dark red. Many vehicles only spent a short time with the company, only being operated for about twelve months before being sold.

In January 1966, Mr Cantello acquired another business when Gee and Harrison Limited of Whittington was taken-over. This included 13 coaches and nine licences for works services to Lea Marston. Most of the vehicles, and the licences had originated with Jackson's Coaches of Castle Bromwich who had previously been taken-over by Gee and Harrison. Radley Motor's livery was grey and light blue but the ex-Jackson's vehicles continued to be operated in that operator's livery of two-tone green.

In September 1966, the Radley Motors fleet was moved to a temporary base at Lea Marston service station before moving to a new purpose-built depot at 10 Fortnum Close in Tile Cross.

The Superb Coaches fleet also moved to this location.

In 1969 Mason's Coachways of Darlaston was acquired and quickly re-named "Mason's - Superb". This company had been started in 1929 by F G Mason and at the time of the take-over operated around five vehicles - four coaches and one double-deck bus. In November 1969 three additional coaches joined the fleet when Hayes Coaches of Walsall was acquired.

During 1970 and 1971 CF Cantello placed six new Caetano bodied coaches into the Masons fleet. The livery of these vehicles was of gold and dark red - identical to Birmingham based Superb Coaches whose fleet had also received many new coaches in the same period.

Until 1973 the operations of Radley Motors and Superb Coaches (Birmingham) were run separate, but two fleets were however merged in that year and all vehicles were licensed to Superb Coaches, although many vehicles displayed both fleetnames. Allenways purchased the combined operations from Mr Cantello in 1973 and continued to operate the Superb Coaches Fleet separate from their own until 1975. Photographs representing the former Radley Motors, Superb Coaches and Mason's Coachways follow on the next few pages.

Radley Motors RRE 453, a 1949 Leyland PS1/1 chassis with 35-seat Bellhouse Hartwell body. This coach was the second vehicle purchased by CF Cantello and was acquired in 1956 from Mainwaring of Audley. PM Photography

Radley Motors HCG 255, 1949 Guy Vixen with 29-seat Wadham body - acquired in 1957 from Aston, Marton. PM Photography

Radley Motors FDW 251, a 1949 Crossley SD42 chassis with 33-seat Plaxton body. This coach was acquired in November 1959 from another Birmingham operator; Hancock's Tours - a small concern that operated with the fleet name of "Comet". PM Photography

Radley Motors VAY 106   the first brand-new coach purchased by CF Cantello. It was the first of two Ford Thames 570E chassis with 41-seat Duple Yeoman bodies acquired in 1960. During 1965 it was one of five coaches transferred to the recently purchased Superb Coaches fleet. RHG Simpson

Radley Motors 145 DOA, a Bedford SB chassis with attractive 41-seat Burlingham Seagull 61 body. This coach was new to the fleet in January 1961 and was followed by two other identical vehicles in August of the same year. RHG Simpson

Radley Motors 437 EOL, one of two Burlingham Seagull bodied Bedford SB chassis to join the fleet in August 1961. This coach is pictured when painted in a plain livery - probably as acquired from the supplying dealer's stock. RHG Simpson

Radley Motors 412 HOH, one of two Bedford SB5 chassis with 41-seat Duple Bella Vega bodies delivered new in 1963. PM Photography

CF Cantello purchased the business of Gee and Harrison of Whittington in January 1966. Thirteen coaches were acquired, nine of which had been new to Jackson's Coaches of Castle Bromwich including ROH 200, a Leyland Tiger Cub with centre entrance Duple Elizabethan body. This was one of a batch of four identical coaches, and of five Leyland Tiger Cubs acquired. PM Photography

The newest of the Tiger Cubs was WOP 600; new in 1958 it had a Duple Britannia body seating 41 passengers. All nine of the former Jackson's vehicles retained that operators two-tone green livery and remained in service with Radley Motors until 1968. RHG Simpson

Radley Motors ROF 500G, one of three Bedford VAM70 chassis with 45-seat Metropolitan bodies acquired new in 1969. Although well established as a bus manufacturer, MCW made attempts in the 1960's to enter the coach body market. The Metropolitan was their most successful with around 40 produced between 1967 and 1969. Omnibus Society collection

Radley Motors ROF 200G, Bedford VAM70 chassis with 45-seat Caetano Cascais body. This was one of eight coaches purchased new for the fleet in 1969. John Mudge

Superb Coaches EUK 783, a 1947 Guy Arab III with Burlingham 33-seat body - acquired from Don Everall of Wolverhampton in 1952. Roy Marshall collection

Superb Coaches DJW 202, a 1942 Leyland TSII with 33-seat Burlingham body - also acquired from Don Everall in 1952. Note the jackets fitted to the radiators of both coaches for winter operation. Roy Marshall collection

Superb Coaches EBA 977, 1950 Foden PVFE6 chassis with 37-seat Plaxton body - acquired from Butlin, Birmingham in March 1957. PM Photography

Superb Coaches EX 7666, a 1953 AEC Regal IV with centre entrance 41-seat body by Gurney Nutting. This unusual coach was acquired from Seagull Coaches of Great Yarmouth in November 1960. PM Photography

Superb Coaches 626 COX, a Burlingham Seagull 61 bodied Ford Thames 570E chassis. This coach was acquired new for the fleet in 1961 and in this view looks very smart in its black and dark red livery. Photobus

Superb used double-deck buses for contract work and a large number, of various makes were operated throughout the years. GKH 698 was a 1943 Guy Arab I with Roe H30/26R bodywork acquired in July 1961 from East Yorkshire and operated until September 1963. Daniel Hill collection

Superb Coaches 928 FOH, Ford Thames 570E chassis with 41-seat Burlingham Gannet body. It was new to the fleet in April 1962. PM Photography

Superb Coaches 766 HOM, Bedford SB5 chassis with 41-seat Plaxton Embassy body. This was one of two acquired new in 1963. PM Photography

Superb Coaches GOP 880D, Bedford VAM70 chassis with 45-seat Plaxton Panorama body. This was one of two new to the fleet in 1966, and of a number of new coaches acquired under the ownership of CF Cantello. Jim Sheldon

Superb Coaches XOC 102J, AEC Reliance chassis with 51-seat Caetano Lisboa body new in 1971. Painted in the 1970's livery of gold, red and black, this coach displays the Radley Motors name on the front destination blind and is pictured when operating on hire to the associated Masons-Superb operation. John Mudge

Mason, Darlaston JDH 858, a Bedford OB, with Duple Vista body, 29-seat, acquired new in June 1946. KAF Brewin

Mason, Darlaston XRE 678, a Guy 6HLW chassis with 41-seat Metalcraft body. This was new to the fleet in 1952 and a similar vehicle was purchased the following year. RHG Simpson

Radley Motors - Fleet list

Reg.	Chassis	Body	Seats	New	Acquired	Sold	Note
JWK 95	Albion CX39N	Bellhouse Hartwell	FC33F	1950	4/56	3/59	Ex Partridge, Coventry
RRE 453	Leyland PS1/1	Bellhouse Hartwell	C35F	1949	11/56	7/58	Ex Mainwaring, Audley
RB 8165	Leyland TS4	Bellhouse Hartwell	C33F	1933	1957	1/58	Ex Superb, Birmingham
HCG 255	Guy Vixen	Wadham	FC29F	1949	12/57	11/58	Ex Aston, Marton
UOB 128	Bedford SBG	Burlingham	C37F	1957	4/58	1/61	Ex Sandwell, Birmingham
GJW 931	Maudslay Marathon 3	Duple	C35F	1949	7/58	11/59	Ex Everall, Wolverhampton
FJN 500	Foden PVRG6	Plaxton	C41C	1952	3/59	1960	Ex Bullock, Cheadale
BEA 32	Daimler COG6	M.C.C.W.	H30/26R	1940	5/59	11/59	Ex Goddard, Birmingham
DKY 510	Daimler CWA6	Duple	H31/26R	1946	11/59	8/61	Ex Davis, Birmingham
FDW 251	Crossley SD42	Plaxton	C33F	1949	11/59	?	Ex Hancock, Birmingham
SEA 750	Bedford SB3	Duple	C41F	1958	12/59	6/60	Ex Hill, West Bromwich
VAY 106	Ford Thames 570E	Duple Yeoman	C41F	1960	4/60	12/65	
3855 HP	" " "	" "	C41F	1960	6/60	3/63	
HTT 328	AEC Regent III	Weyman	H30/26R	1947	10/60	9/63	Ex Dawson, Co. Durham
145 DOA	Bedford SB1	Burlingham Seagull 61	C41F	1961	1/61	1/66	
FDR 53	AEC Regal III	Whitson	C31F	1950	2/61	?	Ex Leighton, Barking
EUJ 118	Bedford OB	Plaxton	FC30F	1948	6/61	6/62	Ex E D Smith, Trench
436 EOL	Bedford SB1	Burlingham Seagull 61	C41F	1961	8/61	8/66	
437 EOL	" "	" " "	C41F	1961	8/61	5/68	
KOD 569	AEC Regent III	Weyman	H30/26R	1949	8/61	6/64	Ex Devon General 569
WUB 987	Bedford SBG	Yeates	C41F	1956	6/62	3/63	Ex Heaps, Leeds
ROE 239	Bedford SBG	Duple	C35F	1955	3/63	7/64	Ex Kunzle, Birmingham
412 HOH	Bedford SB5	Duple Bella Vega	C41F	1963	3/63	1/66	
413 HOH	" "	" " "	C41F	1963	3/63	1/66	
HLX 254	AEC Regent III	Park Royal	H30/26R	1948	9/63	9/63	Ex London Transport RT437
868 MOP	AEC Reliance 2U3RA	Plaxton Panorama	C51F	1964	6/64	12/65	
ROH 100	Leyland PSUC1/2	Duple Elizabethan	C41C	1955	1/66	9/68	Ex Gee & Harrison, Whittington
ROH 200	" "	" "	C41C	1955	1/66	8/68	" " " " "
ROH 300	" ."	" "	C41C	1955	1/66	8/68	" " " " "
ROH 400	" "	" "	C41C	1955	1/66	9/68	" " " " "
WOP 600	Leyland PSUC1/2	Duple Britannia	C41F	1958	1/66	8/68	" " " " "
5422 NX	Bedford SB1	Duple Super Vega	C41F	1960	1/66	2/73	" " " " "
5423 NX	" "	" " "	C41F	1960	1/66	2/73	" " " " "
9259 UE	" "	" " "	C41F	1961	1/66	2/73	" " " " "
9260 UE	" "	" " "	C41F	1961	1/66	2/73	" " " " "
DRF 990B	Bedford VAL14	Duple Vega Major	C52F	1964	1/66	7/68	" " " " "
DRF 991B	" "	" " "	C52F	1964	1/66	7/68	" " " " "
ERF 3B	Bedford SB5	Duple Bella Vega	C41F	1964	1/66	2/73	" " " " "
ERF 4B	Bedford SB13	Duple Bella Vega	C41F	1964	1/66	2/73	" " " " "
4947 NA	Bedford SB3	Duple Super Vega	C41F	1960	1/68	9/68	Ex Dunne, Birmingham
NOG 882F	AEC Reliance 6U3ZR	Plaxton Panorama I	C53F	1968	7/68	2/73	
NOG 883F	" "	" " "	C53F	1968	7/68	2/73	
PBF 931D	Bedford VAM14	Strachan	DP45F	1966	7/68	6/69	Ex Arnold, Tamworth
PBF 932D	" "	"	DP45F	1966	8/68	4/71	" " "
PBF 933D	" "	"	DP45F	1966	8/68	6/69	" " "
PBF 934D	" "	"	DP45F	1966	8/68	6/69	" " "
PBF 935D	" "	"	DP45F	1966	8/68	6/69	" " "
PBF 936D	" "	"	DP45F	1966	8/68	3/71	" " "
JXD 548D	Bedford VAL14	Plaxton Panorama I	C52F	1966	8/68	8/70	Ex Seamarks, Westoning
JXD 547D	" "	" " "	C52F	1966	9/68	1/71	" " "
KCH 105	Leyland PD2/12	M.C.C.W.	H33/26R	1957	10/68	7/72	Ex Trent 762
OTV 195	AEC Regent III	Park Royal	H30/26R	1954	12/68	7/69	Ex Nottingham 195
POA 800G	Bedford VAS5	Plaxton Panorama	C29F	1969	1/69	7/70	
ROF 300G	Bedford VAM70	MCW Metropolitan	C45F	1969	5/69	7/71	
ROF 400G	" "	" "	C45F	1969	5/69	7/71	
ROF 500G	" "	" "	C45F	1969	5/69	7/71	
FJF 175	Leyland PD2/1	Leyland	H33/29R	1950	5/69	5/71	Ex Leicester 136
ROF 200G	Bedford VAM70	Caetano Cascais	C45F	1969	6/69	5/72	
FJF 177	Leyland PD2/1	Leyland	H33/29R	1950	7/69	7/71	Ex Lees, Birmingham
ROJ 900G	AEC Reliance 6MU3R	Caetano Lisboa	C51F	1969	7/69	8/72	
SOB 100H	AEC Reliance 6MU4R	Plaxton Panorama Elite	C45F	1969	8/69	12/72	
SOE 600H	" " "	" " "	C45F	1969	8/69	5/72	
FJF 174	Leyland PD2/1	Leyland	H33/29R	1950	11/69	11/72	Ex Leicester 135

Superb Coaches - Fleet list

Reg.	Chassis	Body	Seats	New	Acquired	Sold	Note
GK 5720	Leyland TS2	Harrington	C32F	1930	3/51	10/51	Ex O A Payne , Birmingham
FV 5851	Leyland TS7	Burlingham	C33R	1935	5/51	11/52	Ex Latham, Longton
ATF 524	" "	"	C32F	1936	8/51	9/52	Ex Harrison, Nuneaton
JOH 296	Commer Commando	Plaxton	C30F	1948	2/52	3/55	Ex Heathcote & Llewellyn, B'ham
JOX 355	Commer Avenger I	Plaxton	C33F	1949	2/52	?	" " " " "
FOF 232	Daimler COG5	M.C.C.W	H30/24R	1939	2/52	9/52	" " " " "
AOG 685	Daimler COG5	E.A. Turner	C33R	1935	4/52	10/52	Ex London Road, Slough
EUK 783	Guy Arab III	Burlingham	C33F	1947	9/52	1955	Ex Everall, Wolverhampton
DJW 202	Leyland TS11	Burlingham	C35F	1942	11/52	1954	" " "
DJW 277	" "	"	C33F	1942	11/52	3/53	" " "
ANX 818	AEC Regal	Harrington	C33F	1936	3/53	?	Ex Meredith, Kidderminster
CTF 741	Leyland TD5C	Burlingham	H30/26R	1938	1953	?	Ex Widnes
EVC 247	Daimler COG5/60	Brush	H29/31R	1940	5/53	7/53	Ex Everall, Wolverhampton
BTD 125	Leyland TD4C	Burlingham	H30/26R	1936	6/53	1956	Ex Widnes
EVC 258	Daimler COG5/60	Brush	H29/31R	1940	7/53	10/54	Ex Everall, Wolverhampton
VV 8912	Daimler CWA6	Duple	H30/26R	1945	10/54	9/58	Ex Northampton 123
GOJ 424	Dennis Lancet	Santus	C33F	1946	1955	1956	Ex Jones, Kings Norton
GH 3802	AEC Regal	Duple	C33F	1931	1955	?	Ex Ideal, Birmingham
NDA 25	Bedford SB0	Burlingham	C36F	1954	8/55	2/57	Ex Everall, Wolverhampton
ADR 800	Leyland TD5	Weyman	L24/24R	1938	1955	3/56	Ex Aston, Marton
RB 8165	Leyland TS4	Bellhouse Hartwell	C33F	1933	1955	9/57	Ex Glossop Carriage Company
OUB 226	Leyland TS7	Burlingham	C33F	?	6/56	5/57	Ex Fell, Barnsley
HOF 740	Leyland PS1/1	Burlingham	C33F	1947	10/56	10/57	Ex Hemmingways, B'ham
JWY 999	Foden PVFE6	Yeates	C39F	1950	2/57	7/58	Ex Partridge, Coventry
EBA 977	Foden PVFE6	Plaxton	FC37F	1950	3/57	1/59	Ex Butlin, Birmingham
VRE 584	AEC Regal III	Yeates	C37F	1951	3/57	1/59	Ex Lymer, Tean
JOH 752	Commer Q4	Nudd	C31F	1949	5/57	5/59	Ex Gallier, Birmingham
EDR 620	Crossley SD42	Whitson	C33F	1948	6/57	?	Ex Pearson, Birmingham
HWB 482	Daimler CWA6	Brush	H30/26R	1945	1/58	1959	Ex Hemmingways, B'ham
KFC 142	AEC Regent II	Park Royal	H30/26R	1946	1/58	12/59	" " "
FOP 467	Daimler CWA6D	Park Royal	H30/26R	1945	1/58	9/58	" " "
ERJ 177	Crossley SD42/9	Plaxton	FC39F	1951	2/58	3/59	Ex Roberts, Crewe
DJW 378	Guy Arab I	Brush	H30/26R	1942	3/58	6/58	Ex Wolverhampton 358
PMB 915	Foden PVRE6	Whitson	C41C	1953	7/58	1/59	Ex Hollingshead, Kent Green
MWL 743	AEC Regal	Duple	C35F	1947	9/58	9/59	Ex South Midland 51
OD 7503	AEC Regent	Brush	H30/26R	1934	9/58	9/59	Ex Lloyd, Nuneaton
KFC 141	AEC Regent II	Park Royal	H30/26R	1946	9/58	12/59	Ex Pugh, Birmingham
HJW 870	Leyland PSU1	Metalcraft	C43C	1950	12/58	10/59	Ex Davis, Birmingham
LOV 35	AEC Regal IV	Burlingham Seagull	C39C	1952	1/59	5/59	Ex Eatonways, Birmingham
LDD 680	AEC Regal IV	Harrington	C41C	1952	3/59	12/59	Ex Tetbury Passenger Transport
GDM 326	Leyland PS2/3	Burlingham	C33F	1951	4/59	11/60	Ex Jones, Ruabon
XOM 186	Morris J2BM	Morris	12	1959	3/59	9/60	
KBA 838	Bedford SB0	Plaxton	C41F	1956	7/59	4/60	Ex Sedgley, Salford
RN 8186	Leyland TD5	ECW	L27/26R	1937	11/59	6/62	Ex Ribble 1802
BWK 155	Daimler COA6	Roe	H31/26R	1936	12/59	11/61	Ex Bailey, Birmingham
ROG 209	Commer Avenger III	Burlingham Seagull	C37F	1955	2/60	7/60	Ex Palmer, Birmingham
189 AOM	Ford Thames 570E	Duple Yeoman	C41F	1960	2/60	11/61	
190 AOM	" " "	" "	C41F	1960	2/60	5/61	
939 BOP	Ford Thames 570E	Burlingham Seagull 60	C41F	1960	7/60	11/62	
YJF 780	Trojan	Trojan	C13F	1960	9/60	6/62	
HEA 433	Sentinal SLC4	Plaxton	C37C	1953	10/60	11/60	Ex Jones, Highhouse
EX 7666	AEC Regal IV	Gurney Nutting	C41C	1953	11/60	3/61	Ex Seagull, Great Yarmouth
626 COX	Ford Thames 570E	Burlingham Seagull 61	C41F	1961	2/61	5/63	
JX 3894	Leyland TS7	Burlingham	C32F	1936	3/61	6/61	Ex Hoyle, Halifax
808 DOK	Ford Thames 570E	Duple Yeoman	C41F	1961	5/61	4/63	
GKH 698	Guy Arab 1	Roe	H30/26R	1943	7/61	9/63	Ex East Yorkshire 402
SDA 163	AEC Reliance MU3RV	Duple	C43F	1956	9/61	5/62	Ex Price, Romsley
KOF 704	AEC Regal III	Burlingham	FC33F	1950	9/61	10/61	Ex Mc.Gill, Aldridge
928 FOH	Ford Thames 570E	Burlingham Gannet	C41F	1962	4/62	11/65	
JPY 112	Bedford SB	Burlingham	C35F	1953	6/62	6/62	Ex Dobson, Bedale
OMB 468	Leyland PS1	Harrington	FC37F	1952	6/62	11/62	Ex Holt, Rochdale
GOE 504	Daimler CVA6	M.C.C.W	II30/24R	1947	6/62	9/63	Ex Birmingham 1504
ROH 7	Commer Avenger III	Plaxton	C41F	1955	1/162	6/63	Ex Myatt, Birmingham
765 HOM	Bedford SB5	Plaxton Embassy	C41F	1963	3/63	4/65	
766 HOM	Bedford SB5	Plaxton Embassy	C41F	1963	3/63	4/65	

Reg.	Chassis	Body	Seats	New	Acquired	Sold	Note
HWP 987	AEC Regal III	Burlingham	FC33F	1950	3/63	5/63	Ex Royal, Redditch
XUX 822	Ford Thames 570E	Burlingham Seagull	C41F	1962	5/63	1/65	Ex Whittle, Highley
NOF 343	AEC Regal IV	Plaxton	C41C	1953	5/63	7/63	Ex Allenways, Birmingham
855 JPT	Ford Thames 570E	Duple Yeoman	C41F	1960	6/63	11/64	Ex Spencer, Manchester
HLX 254	AEC Regent III	Park Royal	H30/26R	1947	9/63	1/67	Ex Cantello, Birmingham
HLW 184	AEC Regent III	Weyman	H30/26R	1947	9/63	1/68	Ex London Transport RT197
HLX 255	" "	"	H30/26R	1947	10/63	7/67	Ex London Transport RT438
KLB 562	AEC Regent III	Park Royal	H30/26R	1950	5/64	1/67	Ex London Transport RT1313
MND 788	Bedford SB	Duple Vega	C33F	1951	5/64	7/64	Ex Blackmore. Coleshill
53 PLG	Ford Thames 570E	Burlingham Seagull 61	C41F	1961	5/64	11/64	" " "
BOX 333C	Bedford SB5	Plaxton	C41F	1965	2/65	1971	
601 JOL	Bedford SB5	Duple	C41F	1963	2/65	1971	Ex Bailey, Birmingham
CON 298C	Bedford CALZ30	Martin Walter	C11F	1965	4/65	4/66	
CON 781C	AEC Reliance 2MU3RA	Plaxton Panorama I	C45F	1965	4/65	6/72	
CON 782C	" " "	" " "	C45F	1965	4/65	2/75	
DOA 382C	Bedford SB5	Plaxton Panorama	C41F	1965	6/65	7/69	
708 RDH	Bedford SB8	Duple Super Vega	C41F	1962	6/65	8/65	Ex Central, Walsall
KLB 889	Leyland 6RT	Leyland	H30/26R	1949	9/65	12/67	Ex London Transport RTW159
868 MOP	AEC Reliance 2U3RA	Plaxton Panorama	C51F	1964	12/65	11/70	Ex Cantello, Birmingham
VAY 106	Ford Thames 570E	Duple Yeoman	C41F	1960	12/65	6/68	" " "
145 DOA	Bedford SB1	Burlingham Seagull 61	C41F	1961	1/66	1/69	" " "
412 HOH	Bedford SB5	Duple Bella Vega	C41F	1963	1/66	5/69	" " "
413 HOH	" "	" " "	C41F	1963	1/66	3/71	" " "
FVP 425D	Bedford J2SZ10	Plaxton Embassy	C20F	1966	4/66	3/69	
GOP 880D	Bedford VAM14	Plaxton Panorama I	C45F	1966	7/66	1/70	
GOP 881D	" "	" "	C45F	1966	7/66	2/70	
436 EOL	Bedford SB1	Burlingham Seagull 61	C41F	1961	8/66	8/68	Ex Cantello, Birmingham
OTV 153	AEC Regent III	Park Royal	H30/26R	1952	1/67	12/68	Ex Nottingham 153
OTV 156	" " "	" "	H30/26R	1952	1/67	1/69	Ex Nottingham 156
EMC 79B	AEC Reliance 2U3RA	Harrington Cavalier	C31F	1964	2/67	9/68	Ex Motorways, London
OTV 198	AEC Regent III	Park Royal	H30/26R	1952	1/68	12/69	Ex Nottingham 198
OTV 197	" " "	" "	H30/26R	1952	2/68	12/69	Ex Nottingham 197
CU 7650	Guy Arab IV	M.C.C.W	H31/28RD	1955	5/69	2/70	Ex Lees, Birmingham
UOL 800H	Bedford VAS5	Caetano Sintra	C29F	1970	6/70	11/72	
UON 700H	AEC Reliance 6MU4R	Caetano Lisboa	C51F	1970	6/70	12/74	
KGK 522	Leyland 6RT	Leyland	H30/26R	1950	9/70	9/71	Ex Stephenson. High Etherley
KLB 948	" "	"	H30/26R	1950	9/70	9/71	" " "
WOC 101J	AEC Reliance 6MU4R	Caetano Lisboa	C45F	1970	10/70	7/73	
950 AFC	AEC Regent V	Park Royal	H30/26RD	1950	1/71	?	Ex Winkle, Willenhall
XOC 104J	Bedford YRQ	Duple Viceroy	C45F	1971	2/71	2/75	
XVK 154	AEC Regent V	Park Royal	H34/28R	?	2/71	12/71	Ex Tyneside PTE
XOC 102J	AEC Reliance 6MU4R	Caetano Lisboa	C51F	1971	3/71	12/74	
XOC 103J	Bedford YRQ	Duple Viceroy	C45F	1971	3/71	2/75	
XOL 105J	" "	" "	C45F	1971	4/71	2/75	
XON 400J	" "	" "	C45F	1971	4/71	2/75	
XOL 300J	" "	" "	C45F	1971	5/71	2/75	
XOV 500J	" "	" "	C45F	1971	5/71	2/75	
BOP 106K	Seddon Pennine IV	Plaxton Panorama Elite II	C53F	1972	2/72	2/75	
COX 600K	" " "	" " " "	C53F	1972	5/72	2/75	
COX 900K	Seddon Pennine IV	Duple Viceroy	C53F	1972	5/72	2/75	
FOC 101L	Seddon Pennine VI	Plaxton Panorama Elite II	C57F	1972	9/72	2/75	
FOC 800L	Bedford VAS5	Plaxton Panorama IV	C29F	1972	9/72	2/75	
FOC 100L	Bedford YRT	Plaxton Elite Express III	C53F	1972	11/72	2/75	
FJF 174	Leyland PD2/1	Leyland	H33/29R	?	11/72	10/73	Ex Cantello, Birmingham
5422 NX	Bedford SB1	Duple Super Vega	C41F	1960	2/73	2/75	" " "
5423 NX	" "	" " "	C41F	1960	2/73	2/75	" " "
9259 UE	" "	" " "	C41F	1961	2/73	2/75	" " "
9260 UE	" "	" " "	C41F	1961	2/73	2/75	" " "
ERF 3B	Bedford SB5	Duple Bella Vega	C41F	1964	2/73	2/75	" " "
ERF 4B	" "	" " "	C41F	1964	2/73	12/73	" " "
NOG 882F	AEC Reliance 6U3ZR	Plaxton Panorama I	C53F	1968	2/73	2/75	" " "
NOG 883F	" " "	" " "	C53F	1968	2/73	2/75	" " "
ROF 200G	Bedford VAM70	Caetano Cascais	C45F	1969	2/73	10/74	" " "

Mason's Coachways - Fleet list

Reg.	Chassis	Body	Seats	New	Acquired	Sold	Note
RF 5874	Karrier 36HP	?	C24D	1929	5/29	1932	Ex Green Garage, Darlaston
WM 4906	Dennis Lancet 1	Spicer	C32F	1932	4/32	11/35	
AOC 15	Dennis Ace	Duple	C20F	1934	5/34	1952	
AOV 698	Dennis Lancet	?	C32F	1935	4/35	9/40	
DOP 511	Dennis Lancet	Dennis	C32F	1938	1/38	9/43	
BEA 259	Crossley PLNFS	Mulliner	C26F	1939	4/40	1952	Ex Favourite I.O.M (DMN 565)
FD 6466	Bean	Willowbrook	C16	1931	5/41	9/42	Ex Field, Dudley
BEA 281	Dennis Ace	?	C26F	1935	7/42	2/53	Ex Favourite I.O.M (MAN 346)
KRE 438	Bedford WTB	Crosbie & Cowley	C26F	1937	9/42	1952	Ex Duggan I.O.M (BMN 237)
KRE 674	" "	" " "	C26F	1937	10/42	?	Ex I.O.M (CMN 76)
GY 9508	AEC Regal	Beadle	FC32R	1932	9/43	1952	Ex Valiant, Ealing
JDH 299	Bedford OWB	Duple	C29F	1945	2/45	11/52	
JDH 858	Bedford OB	Duple Vista	C29F	1946	6/46	3/53	
KDH 99	Crossley CAO	Santus	C30F	1946	1946	?	
KDH 101	" "	" "	C30F	1946	1946	?	
EJW 456	Guy Arab III 5LW	Santus	C33F	1941	5/48	12/57	Ex Everall, Wolverhampton
EJW 458	" "	" "	C33F	1941	5/48	1959	" " "
PRF 167	Bedford OB	Willenhall	FC29C	1948	7/48	5/50	
SRE 326	Crossley CO	Willenhall	C32F	1949	6/49	10/52	
SRE 822	Dennis Lancet III	Santus	C37F	1949	7/49	2/55	
SRE 823	" " "	" "	C37F	1949	7/49	5/59	
GUK 472	Commer Avenger	Plaxton	C33F	1949	9/49	2/56	
HJW 273	Commer Avenger	Santus	C33F	1950	4/50	1/57	
HJW 274	" "	" "	C33F	1950	4/50	1/57	
XRE 678	Guy Arab IV 6HLW	Metalcraft	C41C	1952	6/52	6/58	
YRF 613	" "	" "	C41C	1952	4/53	5/61	Ex Guy Demonstrator
588 KRE	Commer Avenger III	Duple	C41F	1956	4/56	8/63	
587 KRE	" " "	" "	C41F	1956	5/56	7/64	
OOU 739	" " "	" "	C41C	1950	5/58	5/63	Ex Hutfield, Warwick
182 BAX	Ford Thames 570E	Duple Yeoman	C41F	1961	6/63	6/67	Ex Hills, Tredegar
686 SDH	" " "	" " "	C41F	1962	4/64	5/68	Ex hayes, Walsall
4853 DH	Ford Thames 570E	Duple	C41F	1964	6/64	2/69	
CDH 786C	Ford Thames 570E	Duple Trooper	C41F	1965	4/65	4/69	
DDH 568C	" " "	" " "	C41F	1965	5/65	3/72	
GDH 303D	Bedford VAL14	Duple Vega Major	C52F	1966	1/66	5/69	
KLB 917	Leyland 6RT	Leyland	H30/26R	?	7/66	12/70	Ex London Transport
MDH 307E	Bedford VAM5	Duple Viceroy	C45F	1967	1/67	2/75	
NDH 449E	Ford R192	Duple Empress	C45F	1967	3/67	9/71	
TDH 411F	Bedford VAL70	Duple Viceroy	C52F	1968	2/68	9/72	
5200 DH	Ford Thames 570E	Duple Trooper	C41F	1964	11/69	12/70	Ex Hayes, Walsall
COA 396C	" " "	" " "	C41F	1965	11/69	2/71	" " "
HDH 947D	Bedford VAL70	Duple Viceroy	C52F	1966	11/69	3/74	" " "
UON 10H	AEC Reliance 6MU4R	Caetano Lisboa	C51F	1970	1/70	12/74	
WOV 20J	" " "	" " "	C51F	1971	3/71	12/74	
YOF 30J	Bedford YRQ	Caetano Cascais	C45F	1971	5/71	1/72	
YOF 40J	" "	" " "	C45F	1971	5/71	1/72	
YOF 50J	" "	" " "	C45F	1971	6/71	1/72	
YOF 60J	" "	" " "	C45F	1971	6/71	1/72	